# Digital Church Archive

## A to Z Instructions on Planning, Building and Maintaining a Digital Archive Department

## Melvin Barnett

# Table of Contents

# Foreword

It has been my privilege to know and work somewhat with the author of this book, Rev. Melvin Barnett, for several years now. In this book, "Digital Church Archive", he presents a format that will fit any church, large or small, in developing a church website that should help to increase the visibility of the church, without changing its present location.

I first met Melvin when I was serving as the District Elder for the Orangeburg District of the South Carolina Conference of the International Pentecostal Holiness Church. He was living in Florida at that time and had expressed a desire to transfer to South Carolina. Upon arriving in South Carolina he pastored for several years in the Orangeburg District

After our ministry relationship and friendship began to grow, I discovered we had a similar interest. And that was in Archives and Research or the "preserving of history". I had been serving as the Archives Director of the South Carolina Conference for a number of years and Melvin was introducing me to ways of better preserving history as it related to digital preservation.

In one of our annual Archives Seminar in August of 2008, I asked Melvin to share a class with us on the subject of "Putting Together A Church Website". Because of the increased interest and usage of the Internet and websites, I, personally, felt that this subject would enhance the possibilities of our churches in the areas of advertisement and promotion. The idea of creating an Archive Department in each of our churches began to catch fire.

Today, because of the attention given to media, many of our churches now have and use websites which have proven to be an invaluable asset to the growth and success of their local congregations. One aspect of Melvin's presentation that day has been proven true over and over again, "Websites create a digital Archive of Church Information, Sermons and Photographs, as well as creating a Community and Worldwide presence".

I would urge and encourage all of our pastors, local archive directors and church historians to read and benefit from Melvin's latest publication, "Digital Church Archive". This may well change the direction of your church in the media field.

Rev. H. Larry Jones, Pastor St. Paul Pentecostal Holiness Church, Swansea, South Carolina.

South Carolina Conference Archives Director and Executive Council Board Member.

# Preface

A few years ago I was privileged to speak at a 3E Training sponsored by the Discipleship Ministries of the South Carolina Conference of the International Pentecostal Holiness Church, concerning the promotion of media and especially encouraging churches to have an online presence through a website. I remember there just wasn't enough time to get all that should have been said told.

Then in August of 2013, Reverend H. Larry Jones, Conference Archivist asked me to speak during part of his segment of the 3E Training. During this time I specifically spoke on creating a digital archive department in the church. As I prepared for the day of training I realized what a powerful asset this would be in every church, but again there was so much information to convey time wouldn't allow. It was a few days after this event the idea of a book detailing every step of the way was birthed.

I have been privileged to assist many churches, ministries and businesses through the years with their media and online needs. In that time technology has changed drastically. The one positive side of all this change has been the decrease in prices and the availability of so much technology at the disposal of the ordinary Joe.

Thus, my heart was to write a book that not only recognized the need for a more traditional church archive department, but to enhance that department - creating a step-by-step approach to adding a digital archive section that could be visited from anywhere at any time through the power of the internet. Not just any book, but one that would start with the basics and build confidence in people who had no experience with websites or the various programs needed to be successful.

# Acknowledgements

I would like to say thanks to my brother-in-law, Steve Nicola, who many years ago would take time out of his busy schedule to answer a few questions about building websites. I asked as few questions as possible, but his answers made an incredible impact.

I am eternally grateful for one of my greatest friends in life, Pastor Tim Nail, who many years ago invited me to serve Central Chapel as his Executive Pastor and later head up a television ministry. The Church sent me to school which birthed in me a real passion for media in the local church.

More recently, I would like to say thanks to South Carolina Conference Superintendent, Bishop Greg Amos, who invited me to serve as the Director of Media Development. This opportunity has given me a great opportunity to serve in an area of ministry I am very passionate about.

# Introduction

If you're like me, you love to see as well as touch the past. That's why my family and I really enjoy going to historic places and visiting their local museums. Museums are wonderful, but they can come at a real expense to parks and various local historic attractions. Just think of all the great places you have visited and how the collected artifacts and their appropriate display enhanced your whole experience.

Today, more than ever many people are starting to realize how the local church has played a vital role in their community's history as well as shaping its culture. One of the greatest assets to many, especially older churches is its rich history, old records, pictures, and various invaluable items. Such assets are priceless and should never be taken for granted. This is why preserving the past through a proper archive system is important.

We must realize what is not present or future is the past; if we don't take steps to properly preserve it, fading memories are all that will be left before they are soon forgotten all together. In time, accuracy is diluted - as facts become distorted by honest people. Forgetfulness and even prejudice can alter the facts if they are not well preserved with a good, methodical archive system; hence, the vital importance of this book. Now, you too can learn to successfully incorporate an online archive system to preserve historic assets.

The concept and creation of an archive department isn't a huge undertaking, or at least it shouldn't be. While it does take time, coordination, effort and even a little money, with consistent work it is VERY achievable.

In addition to a tangible collection of assets that generally makes up most archive departments, there is the option of adding to your church a digital archive department. In fact, you can start a digital archive department first, and with great success.

The material discussed in this book is intended to teach you how to develop an inexpensive digital archive department in addition to a physical, tangible traditional archive department. As you will read, there are many advantages to creating and maintaining a digital archive department in your local church.

While an archive department is all about the past, the most successful departments understand that the quality and quantity of the pasts' archives begin today where strategic plans are prepared and followed through for the future. Today is the day not only to go back to collect, but to plan for a successful archive department for tomorrow.

By following some simple steps, securing information and purchasing a few items, this simple book can put you on the road to creating an invaluable digital archive department in your church, ministry, business and/or civic organization.

# 1 |The Digital Archive Advantage

## Talking Points

There are some simple advantages to creating a digital archive department in your church. This chapter explains some basic advantages that will give you confidence as well as equip you with talking points to convince others (pastors, boards, committees) of this wonderful option and asset to their church or organization.

I hope these points will both encourage and educate you if you are planning or considering this adventure in your church. The information presented in this book can also be used by other institutions, corporations, non-profits, personal, and family archives.

I use the term, "talking points" very carefully. But, there are ministry opportunities which come around from time to time that do NOT excite others. Often a good, strong presentation coupled with some refreshments is all you will need to garner the support of those less likely inclined toward your ideas.

It is my hope you will have purchased and read this material from cover to cover and more importantly, truly familiarized yourself with the information before making your presentation. You do not want to meet with your Pastor, a board or committee poorly prepared. This ministry is real, and should be a part of any church on some level. Your first line of offense is to convince a few people to get behind you and help. Go ahead and use this resource to determine what you have and the equipment and services you need to purchase; in other words, it's time to count your costs.

Then, make an appointment to present the creation of a digital archive department in your church before your pastor or whomever he designates.

Archives is a ministry, it's a calling, and it requires dedication and long-term commitment. Many people will care less, others will be interested, while a few will actually get in and roll up their sleeves to help.

Below are some "talking points" I have put together to assist you in communicating this potential ministry to those from whom you need support, as well as perhaps a skeptic or two.

There is an old saying, you never get a second chance to make a first impression. So, you may consider creating a presentation with the following points highlighted. This presentation can be digital (PowerPoint, etc.) or put together using some poster board and an easel.

Below, you can go through the talking points and highlight a few details on each slide. The idea is to capture points and then elaborate on each of them. You do not want to present hard-to-read slides filled with lots of details; keep it light and keep it moving though the presentation.

### Easy Setup:
The digital archive department is simple; in this book you have a step-by-step approach to getting started all the way through to a successful functioning archive department. The information and process detailed in this book can be done at people's convenience. Startup can be immediate and build quickly, as people have time to participate.

Before an official presentation to the Pastor or a board, go ahead and have a few people who are willing to help get things rolling. Make sure they can all be at the presentation. You want to convey that you have the necessary support you need to get this ministry off the ground. You do not want to go at this alone if you can help it.

### Minimum Space:
Little space is needed. "Digital" is the keyword. Other than some equipment, the space needed to store all the archive material can fit in the palm of your hand. Backups on hard drives, thumb drives, CDs, DVDs and/or cloud services are highly recommended and very inexpensive.

At worst case, the room and storage for a computer, digital camera, scanner and blank media is the only physical space needed. Most of the time all these items are already in use in a moderate sized church office, and even in many homes. As far as digital storage is concerned, outside of videos, most digital archive departments can fit in a space the size of your thumbnail – literally!

### Minimum Investment:
Most moderate sized churches already own most, if not all the equipment needed. Thus, adding this department comes at little to no additional cost to many churches. When it comes to electronics, the sky is the limit as to what you want to spend; however, creating a digital archive department does NOT require expensive electronic equipment. If you, or your church,

owns a decent computer, digital camera and a scanning device you already own most of what you need.

Most MFC (Multi-Function Copier) type copier/printers have scanning capabilities. Although these scanners are not the highest quality, they will work for scanning documents and old printed photos. A flatbed scanner is the BEST choice. If you have it in your budget to purchase some equipment, I highly recommend the purchase of a flatbed scanner.

### Minimum Liabilities:
Outside of loaned documents and photographs belonging to someone else you have practically no liabilities. To further limit any liability, instead of borrowing items, make an appointment with the person at their home or otherwise agreed place. Let them share their information and/or scan images in their presence. This way, their property never leaves their presence and/or home. Many people are worried about losing or somehow damaging their old photos; this point really puts minds at ease.

### Minimum Maintenance:
Unlike the more traditional archive department, there is little to no maintenance needed. There are no boxes, books and albums to store, shelve, organize and keep dusted. Most digital archive departments will fit on a memory card, stick, or thumb drive, and can be uploaded to a cloud service for safe keeping from fire, flood, theft, and unforeseen accidents.

As for maintenance, the purchase or downloading of a good virus protection program and a means to back up your digital information on the computer is all you need. There are plenty of good, free virus protection programs as well as small, free cloud storage systems. Most of the free cloud storage options are small, but unless you are storing videos may suffice for a good while, if not indefinitely.

I would never trust one place of storage. To be practical, first create a folder on your computer's hard drive and keep all information there; employ the use of sub-folders to keep everything neatly cataloged and searchable. Secondly, upload the folder to cloud storage. Thirdly, spend a few dollars ($5 - $20) on a thumb drive and keep the folder backed up on this device.

### Minimum Training:
The training needed to create and maintain a digital archive department is very simple. Depending on what kind of website or photo sharing service you use, creating this division can be very simple and almost cost free. Young boys and girls can be a real asset to this department because of their

quick grasp of electronic devices. Adult supervision is highly recommended, but children, especially older teens would be a great help for this area of ministry.

As for training, most if not all the software and hardware training can freely be found by searching through your favorite search engine such as Dogpile, Ask, Bing, Google, and Yahoo. YouTube is my favorite place for information, it features millions of videos on everything imaginable.

Another great resource for training is the Goodwill Community Foundation. They have invested in a wonderful program where anyone can freely receive training by going to www.gcflearnfree.org.

### Maximum Exposure:
If you create the digital archive department on a website there are no time limitations and no set hours you must keep. Your digital archive department is available to the public 24/7/365! ALL assets of a digital archive department can be uploaded to a website or photo sharing service. This is the beauty of enhancing an archive department with a digital archive division. As you upload images and documents the department is enlarged, without having to redo the information already available.

Also, all uploads and maintenance is in "real time" or VERY close to it - meaning, that people can visit the website at any time and see the additions as you periodically add them. Once again, there are no hours of operation to keep. The work is immediately available to the visitor as soon as it is uploaded.

## Make a Plan

Getting started is important. A graveyard is the greatest resource of wealth and success, only many of the ideas, ambitions and talents that would have changed a community or even the world simply died. Get together with a few people who are willing to help. Purchase copies of this book and give to each of them. Plan your first meeting. Have your volunteers bring their copy of this book, a notepad, a calendar, and some refreshments, of course.

Set some dates and times to get together and go over what you initially need to do. Get some ideas together before a presentation. Make out some good questions and have answers ready. When you feel confident, plan your first presentation.

If you have already gained support for this ministry but haven't started, the rules still apply. So often I have people say to me, I have always wanted to write a book; what do I need to get started? My exhaustive answer is always the same—start writing. Well, in this case don't just plan, but get together and start. It will come together faster than you think when you start.

## Follow Through

Now that you have planned, it's time to follow through with your plans. In every group of people, very different personalities and gifts will be represented. For example, there are those who are natural leaders, those who encourage, as well as those who are quiet but hardworking. And, then there are some who are not very dependable but are willing to work. Someone needs to lead. A few need to assist the leader, while all the others (majority) must equally be fulfilled in following the leadership.

Everyone needs an assigned job of some kind. It is VERY important to delegate all the load to make everyone feel important and used in the process. No one to three people need to be doing all the work, unless that is all the volunteers you have. A good leadership structure will prove to be a real asset in this process that will truly never end.

Initially there will be lots of calls, legwork and (potentially) - pilfering through old boxes - if your church has been around a while. Remember to take it easy and keep moving forward; after all, Rome wasn't built in a day.

Visit www.melvinbarnett.com for additional information, videos, and examples.

# 2   |What is digital?

WARNING: this chapter may be a little difficult to grasp if you have little to no prior computer knowledge. If you feel overwhelmed after a few paragraphs move ahead and come back later. It all might make even more sense to you then.

From this point on know that everything that is processed and stored on a computer is ultimately compiled of sequences of zeroes and ones, hence the title...Digital Church Archive.

Digital:  1) Of or relating to information that is stored in the form of the numbers 0 and 1.  2) Using or characterized by computer technology.

> "digital." *Merriam-Webster.com*. Merriam-Webster, 2015. Sun. 3 January2015.

Digital is what makes this book unique and the department you are creating so different. The full comprehension of "Digital" is absolutely necessary to understanding most of the concepts, principles, equipment, software, and training discussed in this book.

The "information highway" is no more than billions upon billions, multiplied over and over again, of various sequences of zeroes and ones. These bits and bytes produce everything we sense that is produced by a computer(s), no matter the size or cost.

The mathematical language of using zeroes and ones to communicate is the BINARY language. The sequence of zeros and ones is called binary code. Each zero or one in the binary code represents a "bit." A set of 8 bits (0 or 1) represents a byte (for example: 01000001). A byte is the unit most computers use to represent a character such as a letter, number, or typographic symbol (for example, "a", "8", or "$").

Below is a simple example of how a computer converts the upper and lowercase of the alphabetic characters a, b and c. These are also real examples of a byte.

A: 01000001        a: 01100001

B: 01000010        b: 01100010

C: 01000011          c:  01100011

The point is not to get bogged down in the digital weeds, but rather help you make sense of some common computer lingo you may already use but don't really understand. Or, you may have heard the words tossed around but never understood the meaning, in either case we will briefly explain.

A computer generally comes with a hard drive. The hard drive is measured in bytes. For example, the hard drive in the computer that I am currently using is 450 gigabytes, which is 483,183,820,800 bytes. In short, you can only save the letter "A" (01000001) to my hard drive a little over 483 billion times before you would have to buy another hard drive.

The average word consist of 10 bytes, which makes the typical sentence about 100 bytes. The computer I do most of my work on has a 1 TB (Terabyte) HDD (hard drive), which by today's standards is a normal size. Now, let's put this in perspective, I could put about 1000 copies of the Encyclopedia Britannica on my hard drive or even yet, about 300 hours of quality video.

To give more perspective and add a little computer trivia to the concept, the entire Library of Congress takes up about 10 Terabytes; that would be 10 of my hard drives. Western Digital makes a 10 TB (terabyte) HDD (hard drive) for about $600.00. Yes...that's the whole library stored simply on one inexpensive personal computer.

Everything that is fed into a computer must be digitized, in other words made digital by converting all other formats into zeros and ones, to be processed and or saved. Every song, every picture, every device that is plugged into your computer is digital while being processed. A binary code tells robots what to do. The binary code directs your printer, controls medical equipment such as MRI's. In short the input and the output may be physical, but the process is digital. All these processes are accomplished through bits and sequences of bytes.

Software is the program or instructions that enable hardware to work properly. Ultimately all software comes down to various sequences of zeros and ones also known as machine language. Humans would have a hard time making sense of binary code, so we use programming languages to write software which uses assembly language to convert into machine language.

Each computer processor has its own machine language assembled to give instruction to that particular processor as well as other hardware in the computer.  Each processor is different than the next one unless it is the exact same make and model. This is the reason hardware has to be specifically installed into each computer.

Old Polaroid photos are placed into a scanner as a physical asset, but in moments the scanner digitizes the image, reproducing the image as a digital file to be stored on a memory device. Old cassette tapes can quickly be fed into your mic-in port, played and digitally re-mastered and saved to a memory device. All of which were a physical asset now turned digital.

The re-mastered cassette or the Polaroid photo is now no more than a huge block of zeros and ones that can be reproduced in moments and sent all over the globe in seconds without you ever leaving your chair. The quality is just as pure, if not better. The distribution is endless and free for all practical purposes.

Like many things in life uniformity is necessary to understanding and creating across the board functionality. The digital world is standardized by the quantity of bytes used. When referring to the size of space or quantity of memory used or available this standard is measured in Bytes, Kilobytes, Megabytes, Gigabytes, Terabytes and Petabytes. The chart below illustrates the point I am asserting.

Below is a breakdown of the byte measurements:

| | |
|---|---|
| 8 bits = 1 Byte | Size in Bytes below: |
| 1024 bytes = 1 Kilobyte (KB) | Kilobyte (KB) = 1,024 |
| 1024 kilobytes = 1 Megabyte (MB) | Megabyte (MB) = 1,048,576 |
| 1024 megabytes = 1 Gigabyte (GB) | Gigabyte (GB) = 1,073,741,824 |
| 1024 gigabytes = 1 Terabyte (TB) | Terabyte (TB) = 1,099,511,627,776 |
| 1024 terabytes = 1 Petabyte (PB) | Petabyte (PB) = 1,125,899,906,842,624 |

As you see, the above breakdown lends some explanation to common computer terms you may hear every day but didn't have a grasp of. Just remember, everything going on in your computer is digital, therefore whether its email, websites, social media, pictures, music and the programs it takes to view or listen to the files they are all a string of zeros and ones.

In closing, we often associate some of the above terms with computer hardware such as RAM, Hard Drive space, and virtual memory. One could look at this memory and its common function much like you would a work desk.

The typical work desk consist of a work space (top of desk). Below the center of the workspace is a small drawer that usually runs a good portion of the length of the desk. On the side of the desk is several drawers where other items or files are stored.

The top of the desk represents RAM. Your current project is generally spread out on the top of the desk, as you finish that project it is put away, back into the file drawer, so you can prepare for the next item of business.

The file drawers represent the Hard Drive (HDD). As you clear the desktop, each project is finished or put away for a later date by filing it in the drawers below the desktop.

The small thin drawer under the desktop represents the Virtual Memory. As you know, everything doesn't fit on the desktop, so you store quick retrievable items conveniently in this drawer that assist you with the desktop. You might store extra pens, stapler, a hole-punch, extra paper clips and such in this area.

The physical memory of a computer is very much like the example above. In short all (digital) data has to be processed and stored in bytes.

Visit www.melvinbarnett.com for additional information, videos, and examples.

# 3 | Equipment Needed

All jobs require tools; the digital archive department is no exception. Many churches and homes already own much, if not all the tools and equipment needed for the development, building, and maintenance of this new department. Below; you will find a list of equipment needed for this mission.

## Computer

The computer is the backbone of the digital archive. It is the primary component of the equipment you will need. You need a good quality computer, but not necessarily a brand new one or even the latest model. This section of the chapter gives good instruction and recommendation on what you will need to accomplish the mission of building and maintaining your digital archives.

### Purchasing a computer

If you already own a good computer you can skip this section; however, if you're going to buy one perhaps this section of the chapter will come as a benefit to you. I have divided this section up into five points you should consider before the actual purchase.

Computers are like automobiles, furniture and jewelry; they are always on sale, so do NOT be bamboozled into making a purchase by a high pressure salesperson. Be mentally prepared to walk out of a retail store if the salesperson can't get prices where you want them as long as your expectations are based on the current market.

Take your time and do the research. Your computer will serve as the BACKBONE of your digital archive department; therefore, make a wise informed purchase. Be careful – sometimes money can be wasted when you're trying to save a dime. Every ASSET of your digital archives will pass through this computer. Buy smart the first time!

### *Laptop or desktop?*

Where are you going to set up an office to create and maintain your digital archive department? Will you operate from your home? Or perhaps you have an office designated on the church or ministry properties. Bottom line, if you know you have a steady place to do your work you should go with a desktop. Why? Expandability. Functionality. Economics. More bang for the buck. Better all-around workspace creating better workflow.

A laptop will give you mobility, especially if there is no place to have an office or at least a semi workspace. Mobility requires the storage, transportation and connection of the external peripheral devices such as a printer and scanner. Connecting, disconnecting, storage and transportation of devices can take a real toll on the life of your equipment.

For newer equipment boasting the latest hardware configurations, a desktop will be cheaper than a laptop. However, don't get sucked into buying the latest technology; let others pay that high cost of R&D.. Stick to technology six months to a year old and you will save half the money.

### Shop Around

When it comes to buying a computer I'm not much on patronizing. HP, DELL, Acer, Asus, or Gateway to name a few, are all the same sitting on a store shelf. The fact is, you may find it hard to find certain models at every store; however, the hardware configuration could be the same or very close.

Some of your large "Big Tent" stores buy in such volume that manufactures will sell them a bulk of systems that are configured or modeled differently. So, the salesperson can tell you, "We are the only store that sells this model." In other words, a manufacturer may not configure a dime of difference between a system sold in Walmart, Best Buy or Office Depot, but they ALL have different specifications when you look at the fine print. So do the leg work, shop around, and find the best price on the "same" system.

Before buying a computer I would start a good online search. Go online to all the major electronic stores and department stores. Look and compare hardware configurations. The Sunday paper is also a good place to find weekly ads with some great prices. Remember, many merchants will match prices of the same system or those that are VERY similar – use price matching to your advantage. But, be careful of high cost warranties. We will discuss warranties later.

Computer technology changes every month as does the price for the equipment. It would be easy to cite the facts and figures of a good computer, but tomorrow my information may be obsolete. As the market changes so does the demand for hardware and software. A good salesperson (who is not on a commission) can often point you to the right machine if you are forthcoming with your needs.

In addition to relying on a salesperson, consider Googling for computer reviews and what you will need the computer for. While there is a lot of junk on the Internet, there is a wealth of information to help you make an educated decision about this whole process.

Buying online is also a great idea. I have successfully purchased most of my computers and peripheral devices online, saving piles of money! Even if you buy online from Walmart or Target, you are likely to save money over walking into the store. Also, NEVER pay shipping – there's too much competition to pay someone shipping for a big ticket item.

In a lot of industries, proprietors have figured sneaky ways to boost revenue; electronic equipment is no different. While I hate purchasing warranties, I find myself buying them when it comes to computers and equipment. The key is not to be a sucker. Warranties and/or maintenance plans should be a part of the whole budget consideration.

Years ago I went to buy a laptop from a well-known "big tent" electronic store, one that I can spend hours perusing even today. The laptop I picked out was great! Full of features and relatively newer technology, it was kind of like, "too good to be true." When I got the system up to the counter and I soon learned that the 2-year extended warranty was half the price of the laptop. This was a NO SALE! To me this is a scam that is perpetrated on consumers every day - and it is legal.

Fortunately, because of the high price of warranties, some of the big online stores offer warranties based on the cost of the equipment. Often these warranties are full replacements of merchandise. This is why I have become such a fan of buying from Amazon and Walmart online.

### New, used or refurbished?
Hey, here's an option to help save a little money - buy used or refurbished equipment. You can often purchase "open box" items that carry the same warranty as new. When shopping around be sure to ask the salesperson for open box, or refurbished equipment; there is no shame in doing this. Many online stores have a refurbished area of their website. I have had some good luck with these purchases.

### Never buy top of the line
Let's keep this simple! If you buy the top of the line, most recent equipment, you are going to have to help the manufacturer recover research and development costs. These costs are going to be paid by the consumer for months, if not a year or more. It is okay to purchase technology that is 6

months to a year old, without any reservation. I have done it for years—it's just smart and saves about 50% in costs.

### RAM is important

I will explain RAM (Random Access Memory) in detail later, but to cut to the chase, RAM is important. You want to buy as much RAM as you can afford. The trick is, when you look at some seemingly inexpensive systems watch out for RAM deficient systems marked down to sell quickly. Here is a good rule of thumb, familiarize yourself with the prices of computer systems from cheap to expensive. Then notice the amount of RAM being used in the middle priced systems. You should buy or have installed that amount of RAM if you can afford it.

### Conclusion

When you have picked the system you want, you need to pay close attention to the costs, the shipping and warranties. Listen, I love supporting a local economy. I also like going to a big tent department store where I can see and touch the merchandise as well as talk with a salesperson, but in today's economy making decisions often depend on pros and cons, gains and losses, and weighing out the overall benefits. As for me, I love the free shipping, bottom price and a good, cheap warranty. Thus, I spend a lot of money online.

If you value home town (local) spending over ordering online plan to spend 15% to 25% more for the same computer system. Local purchases have the value of good service when you need help... and that has plenty of value which could be a wash over ordering online.

## Minimum computer requirements

### Processor

The processor is the brain of the computer. Today's market generally offers two choices, AMD or Intel. In short AMD will always save you money. Apples to apples, AMD systems are very dependable, last for years, and save money upfront. Intel makes a great processor as well. People can argue the difference and there are plenty of them, but for surfing the Internet, building a website, photo editing, video and audio editing, the AMD will work fine.

If you plan to do extensive video editing you might consider an Intel processor—it just simply out performs its AMD counterpart. Stay with an AMD, and you will do well and save money. Processors have speeds measured in Gigahertz (GHz). You want to stick with something around 2.0 GHz or higher. Also, new software is being developed every day for 64 bit architecture so don't waste your money on a 32 bit system.

### RAM

RAM is the next big investment. I wouldn't invest in a system with less than 8 GB of RAM preferable DDR-3. You want fast memory and plenty of it. 16 GB of RAM would provide a nice seamless experience when editing photos, audios and videos. With 16 GB of RAM and a decent quad core processor, you won't be waiting on your computer.

RAM will make a noticeable difference in your speed if you are short changed. Do not cut corners on RAM, make sure you have plenty, you will not regret this decision.

### Graphics

Graphics is important to maintaining a digital archive department. Generally speaking most people aren't worried about the graphics card in their computer. Simply said, if you can, purchase an average to above average graphics card with plenty of memory, especially if you intend to edit videos, otherwise a standard card shouldn't be a problem.

Most computers have what is an integrated graphics card, this means it is built into the motherboard, not a separate item that is plugged into a card slot in the back of your system. If you do want to purchase an additional card for better performance you can purchase one that simply by-passes the integrated system once it is plugged into the system. For most users a secondary purchase of a graphics card isn't warranted.

### Ports

The more the better. You want plenty of USB-3.0 ports. I wouldn't buy a machine with less than 4 USB (at least two USB-3.0) ports in the back no matter how many they stuck in the front of the machine. Add two more USB ports to the front for a minimum of 6 USB ports. You want 3 rear audio jacks, plus a speaker jack in the front and an Ethernet port for hardwiring into a network or the Internet. A card reader is a plus; this gives you the option of plugging your digital camera's memory card right into the computer.

### Hard Drive

If you can, go with something at least 850 GB or bigger running at 7200 RPM. Video is VERY demanding on hard drive (HDD) space. If you plan to add lots of video to your digital archives you want to purchase a least a 1 TB HDD.

If you have it in your budget, the new solid state hard drives are so fast you never have to wait. Even the boot-up process when you turn your computer on is lightning fast. It's not a necessary item, but it is fast.

### Monitor

Monitors are tricky. A good buy may not be a good fit for your system if you are going to be editing photos and videos, especially if you are really serious. If you have a laptop then options are limited. If you want a quality monitor for editing go with a matte finish (as opposed to a glossy screen) IPS LED monitor. The LCD is usually a little cheaper.

### Software

I pay little attention to the software that comes on a computer. If you can get a good deal on MS Office then perhaps consider purchasing it. A good bit of the preinstalled software is junk! I generally take a few hours when setting up a computer for the first time to remove all the junk and trial version software.

Be careful deleting software, but trial version stuff can usually be deleted. Also, go ahead and get rid of all the Internet providers (which I will not name) and virus programs. There are plenty of good FREE virus protection programs that are safe and protect well.

Also, Microsoft is notorious for shoving Internet Explorer with all kinds of junk in the toolbar. Every search engine wants to highjack your system to steer you in their markets. Turn these off or delete them, if possible.

Microsoft Office is a good product if you can afford it. Then there is the OpenOffice which is free and a VERY powerful program.

In short you need a good anti-virus program, a word processor, email server, browser, photo editing program, audio editing program and, if editing video, a video editing program, as well. Next, depending on the route you take, you may need a good HTML editor for building websites from scratch.

### Video options

Editing video requires a larger and faster processor, graphics capability, memory (RAM) and certainly a good sized hard drive. Video files are LARGE, they take up a lot of space on hard drives. A good sized hard drive is a real asset. Many of the new desktops come with ample to nearly ample space. If you have the option of increasing the hard drive space I would highly suggest doing so, if you know you will be adding a fair amount of videos to your digital archive department.

Often, choosing to enlarge the hard drive at the time of configuration and/or purchase outweighs the cost of adding a second one or replacing the one that came with the system.

### Audio options

Editing audio (sermons) isn't as taxing on a computer system as editing video. Generally, outside of the appropriate software there is little extra equipment needed.

In short, all audio files need to convert to Mp3 or an acceptable format. Some of the newer sound equipment used in churches has the ability to properly compress and write directly to an acceptable format.

The right audio software will give you the ability to re-record over bad audio, by removing hiss, amplifying low signals and equalizing the content. However, the real asset is having the capacity to edit by doing voice-overs, such as adding introductions to the selected audio file.

Editing gives you the ability to take an audio file and add pertinent information that will permanently be part of the new mastered file.

For example, I have run across many old cassettes that barely had the sermon title, date and minister's name still visible. Sometimes there may be some significant purpose to the recording. Through audio software, you can preserve all this information by adding it to the recording at the beginning and/or end when you re-master the recording.

We will go deeper into software in another chapter.

# Headphones

I would highly suggest purchasing a good quality pair of headphones to edit and produce audio and video. Unless you spend some money, the speakers that came with your computer are poor to fair in performance. While I have good speakers, BOSE, I depend on a good quality set of earphones when editing audio. Headphones can be very expensive; but before you waste a lot of money I would like to suggest a pair of studio headphones such as the Behringer HPS3000. You can get them for about $20.00 +/-. I own two pair and use them all the time. Even a pair of simple IPod or Mp3 headphones is better than using external speakers. Full ear coverage is the best.

Headphones brings the audio signal straight to your ears as opposed to all the noise that can contaminate a signal from the distance of your speakers to your ears. This point cannot be stressed enough. There is a reason that no matter how grand a recording studio is built, everyone still wears headphones when recording.

When editing audio, there is often hiss and background noise that can be quickly eliminated from your recording. You also want to shut off all external noise such as outside traffic, ticking clocks, electronic white noise such as micro fans running to cool equipment, humming equipment, lights, the AC or heater kicking on and off, children playing, doors closing, and sinks and toilets running. These are just a few irritants I have listed.

## Digital Camera

Use of a digital camera is a must. They are affordable; and simply deleting bad images is quick and free of cost. As far as cost - you can purchase a small, but decent camera for about $60. As far as how much you want to spend on a camera, the sky is the limit. If your budget will allow, you can purchase a nice Canon entry level DSLR kit for about $600 - $700. This kit would be a great asset to your digital archive department.

A lot of people are now using IPads, tablets and Smartphones to take photos. While the megapixels are increasing in size, the camera's sensor is still very small and CANNOT produce the same quality image as a decent, standalone digital camera. While phones, tablets and such are handy to snap photos in some cases, I would not intentionally use these devices as a means of capturing photos for archival use. And, I wouldn't spend more than one minute with a salesperson trying to steer you in this direction. Go ahead and purchase a standalone point and shoot, or if funds are available, a DSLR camera.

I am a Canon guy myself, but there are some really great affordable brands to choose from which will produce wonderful results. If you want to incorporate video into your digital camera, $200 - $250 will purchase a decent brand (Canon, Nikon, Samsung, etc.), even in 1080p High Definition. The key to a purchase is research and reading reviews.

Generally speaking, the photographer, not the camera, is the weakest link in capturing great photos. A few hours of watching photography tips on YouTube will yield amazing results. I would steer clear of getting roped into taking an online photography class. There is way too much free assistance through blogs and various videos online.

The key to a getting the digital archive department started is collecting photos/videos and having people record events sponsored by your church.

Often in a moderate sized church there are people who already have a love for photography; use them to take photos. Most likely, they already enjoy photography and are most likely fair to good at it, as well.

If there is someone in your church who loves photography, they can often save the church from having to buy a camera to start with, or at least postpone the expense. In such cases, it would be helpful, at the least, to furnish them with batteries, if they are using an external flash. Or, you can give them a monetary gift from time to time to go toward new camera gear. This approach can save the church money as well as liabilities on the church's part. An in-house photographer might be willing to edit the photos they take for website use, especially if you let them display their contact and company information in an appropriate manner.

In purchasing a digital camera, please do not get caught up in the whole megapixel race. Lately, many camera manufacturers have been releasing cameras, smartphones and tablets that have huge megapixel sizes, but actually produce poor images. Megapixels are measured in how many pixels can be placed on the camera's sensor. The more megapixels the larger the picture can be increased without demonstrating noise due to cropping. However, a decent DSLR has a much larger sensor than a smartphone, or tablet; thus, a great sensor with only 8 megapixels is better than all phones, tablets and such.

A small camera, tablet or smartphone uses a very small sensor, so no matter how high the megapixel, you can't get enough light into the sensor to produce a great photo. For example, the IPhone 5 has an 8 megapixel camera using a 4.54mm x 3.42mm sensor with an aperture of f/2.4. If a person was oblivious to the sensor size - a few years ago this would have been a great camera to shoot an indoor wedding. The only problem is the pictures would be terrible because there just isn't enough space on the sensor to absorb the light and produce the quality.

On the other hand, I have a Canon EOS 20D. It is also an 8 megapixel camera, but the sensor is 22.5mm x 15mm. These specifications, coupled with an f/2.8 aperture lens have produced stunning wedding photographs. To sum up my point - don't get caught up with all the megapixels without weighing out the size of the sensor.

## Scanner

A scanner is not optional; it is required, in my opinion. If you have old photos and documents such as old ledgers, bulletins, flyers, records and such, you can easily scan the data in and add them to your digital archive department. It's possible your church may already own a scanner. Many MFC's (multi-functional copiers), and all-in-one machines have scanner capabilities; however, unless it is a stand-alone scanner, the quality will not be as good.

Once again, I am a Canon guy. A Canon or Epson scanner can cost anywhere from $60 - $200. Resolution (or DPI) is the most important element to look for in a scanner. You should stay above 6400 DPI, preferably 9600 DPI resolution, when making this purchase.

The stand-alone flat-bed scanner usually interfaces with many photo editing software programs allowing you to scan an image right into the program for editing. Most of the time older, scanned, printed photographs need editing, and a lot of it. Faded photographs can be restored. Scratched photos can often be fixed. Colors saturated to create a better more vivid image is a quick process. Images can easily and quickly sharpened.

To limit liabilities, I suggest if someone wants to contribute photos or documents to the church, have them bring the articles to the church. Or, if you are using a laptop, take the computer and scanner (don't forget a 12 ft. extension cord) to their residence and scan the items onto the hard drive; enjoy the visit and go home or back to the office and edit the images.

If you own a laptop, but use a desktop for editing, you can often copy your software and drivers onto the laptop for portability, thus allowing you to do field work.

Many people feel more comfortable if they are in the presence of their protected photos. Inviting them to the scanning event or using a laptop to visit their home may put their minds to rest about your losing their photographs.

Last, but not least, some of your more expensive scanners come with some great photo editing software, such as Adobe Photoshop Elements. Epson is rumored to have some good photo editing software in the box as well. As I stated, you generally have to spend a little more money to get good software, but the higher price may be cheaper in the long run, if great software such as Adobe Photoshop Elements is included. Photoshop Elements alone will cost you between $90 and $120.

## File Storage

You must have a backup plan for your digital archive department. In a split second a hard drive can fail and you are eternally out of ALL your hard work just that quickly. For most digital archive departments a storage solution is simple and inexpensive. However, there are several routes you can take; I recommend both local and cloud. First, local storage such as CDs, DVDs or thumb drives may be the cheapest way out, instead of using a cloud service. You can buy a 32GB flash (thumb) drive for about $20.

Depending on the size of megapixel your camera produces and the end product of your editing, you can get a lot of storage for $20. For example, a 32GB thumb drive will hold about 7,639 images (JPEG at 100% quality) at 12 megapixels each. As for RAW, you can get up to 1,280 images on the same thumb drive.

Another viable option is to purchase an external USB hard drive. For about $60 you can purchase a 1 TB (terabyte) hard drive. Cloud service can be pricey if you use a lot of space. Thus, purchasing an external hard drive and keeping it at a different location from your computer is a really great plan. If you are going to upload videos and a lot of audio sermons, you will need an external hard drive rather than a thumb drive.

The good thing about an external hard drive is - it is inexpensive and very dependable. I personally use a USB 1 TB WD (Western Digital) Passport. I purchased it, along with a separate, hard nylon case, for $75.88. I researched the options and read over many reviews. This product came in at a 4.4 out of 5.0 with the reviews—nothing is perfect. This hard drive is extremely portable and doesn't need an external power source, because it is powered through the device when plugged into a USB port. The physical size (4.25" x 3.25" x .75") is perfect. There are other great brands to use; just study the reviews real closely and feel comfortable about your decision.

A serious digital archive department can rack up a lot of files and photos that will slowly eat away at your memory. I have a lot of photos; at last count I had 123GB in just photos, 8.7 GB in music, and 1.58GB in website material on my PC.

While an external hard drive is the best short and long-term solution, the safest and surest solution is backing up your files on disks (CDs or DVDs) and storing them in a cool, dry, fire-proof safe. If you are just starting a digital archive department at your church, most likely backing up data on a DVD will work for a long time, if you keep things simple.

For unforeseen reasons, such as theft, fire, flood or acts of God, I would always store your backup separately from the computer, as in separate buildings. Perhaps, keep one at the church and the other at the parsonage or some other home or place of business. Always plan for a computer crash or hard drive failure and you will never be sorry.

Many people are resorting to cloud storage services. This is a remote backup system you upload through the Internet. Many computer manufacturers are offering free cloud storage for their own devices, but the space is limited. Google, Amazon, Apple and others offer some space; you can always purchase additional space, if needed. There are also great third party vendors you can purchase cloud service through, often saving money. ichurchweb.com offers great cloud storage plans that are VERY affordable, as well as one stop shopping for domains, email, hosting, and website products.

Reliability is the key to these services. While checking these options, be sure to check out ichurchweb.com products and services. They are beautifully priced and I trust them to deliver quality every day. They have a toll free number, they are open 24 / 7 / 365, and Tech Support is located here in the States.

One of the biggest mistakes I see people make when backing up their files and folders is under using the space on their media. I would personally use DVD over CD for storage. A DVD holds about 4.7GB while a CD, only holds about 650MB or 74 minutes of audio. There is no need in putting various photos on multiple DVDs or CDs. If the media fails it will completely fail to view 1 photo or 500 photos. I do not suggest stuffing a media source to capacity, but at least fill it 80% of the way.

## Cloud Storage and Integration

There is a lot of buzz about cloud storage and cloud based software. Lately, many software giants are developing cloud based programs. They work much like a secure website. The push is to ultimately sync software, user files and personal settings in the cloud all the while producing a seamless experience no matter where you are and no matter what device you are using whether it's a tablet, smartphone or a desktop at work.

For example, I use Microsoft Office 365, OneDrive, OneNote all synced on my smartphone, tablet and two desktops - all with a cloud storage of 1 Terabyte. When I open OneNote and add information it is available in real-time on my cell phone. While all this sounds great there is one common denominator that links all this together and often the quality of service along with the security is anyone's guess—Wi-Fi.

Google has entered the race with some really nice as well as very powerful products that integrate all platforms and devices. I use a few of them as well. They have the convenience of being free for most users. The integration between Windows and Android has proven to be pretty smooth to say the least.

Last, but not least, you have Apple tearing the consumer market up with a host of nifty devices that integrate between each other. These products are a little pricey, but are user friendly and offer some great software options that will work for a digital archive department.

While the world has celebrated the ease of having so much technology at their fingertips, seamlessly integrated across so many devices and platforms, they are dependent on Wi-Fi to connect them to the cloud.

Exploitation, compromise and destruction of the "cloud" is the next generation of warfare on earth. Civilized countries have already begun to develop strategies to defend themselves against "Cyber Warfare."

Over the Christmas Holidays of 2014, millions of people's credit card and personal information was stolen.

Recently, it was discovered that the U.S. Department of Defense authorized a virus to be planted into Iran's Nuclear reactors.

As millions of people sync their smartphones with their laptops, tablets and desktops, many of those apps are absolutely dangerous and are actively mining for all kinds of personal information. I was reading that recently a large bank security agency confirmed that many of the popular flashlight apps are developed in communist and state sponsored terrorist countries. Upon loading the app you give them access to your contacts, media, phone list, SMS/MMS messaging, camera, voice recorder and GPS location just to name a few—Why?

We hear of cyber criminals hacking into Facebook, Google, large banks, Insurance companies, department stores and other enterprises on a weekly basis. All these crimes have the same thing in common, your data being connected all over the world through the internet and generally accessible through a local network or Wi-Fi connection.

So what is my point? Don't trust the cloud any farther than you can extend your own hands. I suggest real software on a disk that can be re-loaded into your computer when it fails. I suggest a real tangible backup plan that you have complete control over at your own finger tips.

I don't sweat the software and their means of delivery and back-up. Like anyone, I get plenty tired of having to wait on or authorize an update on my computers and devices, but personal data and files is my business. "My Documents" is just what they say they are...mine. And, I am responsible for my own backups. I have read the fine print on all the cloud services and none of those services will stand with you two minutes when you have lost every bit of your hard work and late night hours.

Keep a real backup, one that you have control over, one that you can place in your own hands and put where you feel it is safe. Integrate a cloud service as a secondary backup. Use it to go between devices if you want; I do it all the time and it is great, but ultimately all my data gets saved to a local hard drive and then backed up on a physical device. I suggest you adapt the same practice—the sooner the better.

Visit www.melvinbarnett.com for additional information, videos, and examples.

# 4  |Software

## Photo Editing Software

Photographs require editing, therefore, good editing software is a must! Software prices range anywhere from free to about $600. In order to use any decent editing software some basic instruction will be required if you have no prior experience. Even simple free or inexpensive editing software solutions require minimum training. Your depth of computer knowledge may determine how much training you need.

### PC or Mac
For the most part, your choice in editing software depends on whether you are using a PC (Windows) or Mac (Apple).  Statistically speaking, most will be using a PC, so software cost and performance can range from one extreme to another. On the other hand, Macs generally come with decent photo editing software and even a decent, but small, video editing package that is very practical for most amateur users.

### Mac users
Mac generally prides itself in offering some all-around novice software to assist the user in most normal demands. Their software isn't cheap, but it usually works very well, so you get bang for the dollar. The only disadvantage to using a Mac over a PC for establishing a digital archive department is having enough people who are literate in operating a Mac.

Mac certainly sets the bar high when it comes to a graphics environment. The 2014 market shows about 18% of Internet users using a Mac or Apple based product compared to Microsoft Windows (PC) coming in at about 57%. The rest of the people are using Linux based systems such as Android, Kindle or similar products. The purchase and use of Mac products is a good one; however, based upon market share, there is minimum products and instruction to assist you.

### PC (Windows) Users
I personally use Adobe Photoshop Elements; this is a cut-down version of

the full Photoshop - which is now available in a monthly lease for around $10.00. Elements can be purchased outright. You can also buy Adobe Elements combined with a slimmed down version of their professional video editing software known as Adobe Premiere Elements. Buying this combo is VERY cost effective and gives you a wonderful featured editing solution. One word of caution, Adobe is now engaged in the practice of leasing a good bit of their professional software by the month, hence driving up the overall cost tremendously. Be careful and weigh your options first. I am still very skeptical of the whole monthly cost of any software product.

Just to give you an idea of the cost - you can buy Adobe Photoshop Elements 13, for $87.24 though Amazon (9/2014). Or, you can get the combo (Elements 11 and Premiere 11) for $129.99. Most Adobe products come in PC and Mac versions. I have professionally used Adobe Elements in both Windows and Mac systems.

There are other PC and Mac based photo editing programs available for less cost. If you were creating a digital archive department, I would strongly advise working this cost into the budget, if possible. If you are tight on finances perhaps someone could sponsor the product in memory of a friend of family member. The product I use and have suggested will absolutely work for any digital archive department.

Free software is an option, but there are few decent programs out there. The best free photo editing PC software I have seen is Gimp. It is a VERY powerful editing software solution and is absolutely free for the downloading (www.gimp.org). Gimp isn't just a cheap way out; it is a VIABLE solution for photo editing—one that rivals a professional photo/graphics editor.

Gimp has a Mac feel. I personally don't like using it because I feel much more comfortable inside my Windows Photoshop environment, but Gimp is an excellent (FREE) product which I do use from time to time because Elements just can't keep up with a couple of my graphic demands.

One last thing, many decent to professional software programs come with a 30-day free download trial. I would urge you to take advantage of these opportunities, and also to watch some YouTube videos made specifically for your software choice. All the big name photo and video software products have a huge source of "how to" videos on YouTube; take advantage of these resources.

In this chapter I do not intend to give lessons, but to communicate what I know works and has been found to be simple to operate. As stated earlier, some photo editing software comes pre-installed on scanners, cameras, and even some color printers. New PC's generally have a very small photo or paint program that is really useless for anything other than entertaining little children.

In conclusion: Google around, do your research and read plenty of reviews and you might find another great product that works for you. My picks are Gimp (free) and Adobe Photoshop Elements.

## Audio Editing Software

Why do you need an audio editing software? For starters, the industry standards in audio has made its greatest leap in the past two decades. We have seen the VHS as well as the cassette tape disappear before our eyes. Today both audio and video is recorded on the same media.

Older churches generally have a few boxes filled with old cassette tapes of their pastor's messages. These tapes are priceless when it comes to archives. Audio software allows you to re-record them to a stable file format and media. At the same time, you can do voice overs to give information about the person or message on the cassette before and/or after the content.

You can also take a recorded CD of the service and produce it by adding an introduction such as some music and vital information about the church, pastor, service times, address and other special information that would not have recorded with the message or event, but you now want communicated to the listener.

Editing audio files is simple once you learn the software and workflow. Once the audio is edited you can compress it into an Mp3 and upload straight to your website or produce a master CD and mass produce it in a duplicator all in an hour, if you work at it.

### Paid Audio Software

For years now, I have used Sony products to edit my audio. I like them because I find them simple and they meet my editing needs. However, there are other great and even better software products out there for the job. I guess it's all in what you get used to, and that holds true for most software use. I tend to trust Sony, Adobe, Microsoft and most Apple brand software.

Before making a purchase, know what you want to do with the software. Rid yourself of any product that can't do the job. Find a simple product that does all you need to do (at a great price) and download a trial version, if they offer it. Generally, trial versions run about thirty days and more often than not, they have a few limitations.

**Below is a list of great audio software products that review really well:**

- Ableton Live: Medium to Expert
- Image-Line Fruity Loops: Beginner and up
- Apple Logic Pro: Medium to expert
- Avid Pro Tools: Professional
- Propellerhead Reason: Medium
- Apple Garage Band: Beginner and up.
- Sony Acid (Music Studio): Beginner and up.
- Steinberg Cubase: Medium to expert.
- Cockos Reaper: Beginner and up.
- PreSonus Studio: Medium to expert.

## Free Audio Software

Below is a list of great FREE programs for your audio editing. I have only used one of these programs but they are rated well in reviews. I would take time to download some of them and see for yourself. You might consider doing some research online to help you rule out some of the programs that will not work for your need.

- Wavosaur
- Waveshop
- Acoustica Basic Edition
- MP3Gain
- Audacity
- Music Editor Free
- MP3 Quality Modifier
- Wavepad
- Mp3DirectCut

# Website Editing Software

### Online Web Builders
Today, many website host offer WYSIWYG (What You See Is What You Get) online site builders. These are very easy, and take little time, to figure out. They are also very powerful and generally offer a lot of trendy services and a huge variety of templates so you can immediately get started building an awesome website. For the most part, there is no prior experience needed, just a lot of creativity and a willingness to follow directions.

The online web builders can make a creative minded beginner look like a pro. As I said, they are usually very easy to figure out. The key is to be very patient when getting started. I find that the best thing to do is tinker around with the online builder. Don't get started building a site until you feel comfortable using the program with results you have commanded. Also, be sure to check for online tutorials using the builder of your choice.

Most large domain and hosting providers offer their own online builder. Among the good providers, I recommend using products found at www.ichurchweb.com, they offer many templates to get you up and running in minutes.

### Disadvantage of online web builders
Generally speaking, most of the larger webhost services offer their own web builder program. However, be forewarned of a huge disadvantage to using an online web builder. If and when you ever decide to move your website, none of your hard work and countless hours of blood, sweat and tears are transferable. Simply stated, you lose ALL your work and have to start over from scratch. Now, of course you will hopefully have all your photos and such backed up on a computer. You will only lose what you have uploaded.

I have seen this happen to many people in the past and it is a very sad day. Therefore, it is good to use a web editor where you upload your website instead of creating a website through their proprietary online builder. With this said, there are some good webhost services that have stood the test of time. They will be around for many more years to come and the possibilities of losing your data is unlikely.

Some other discouraging factors to consider are: prices may change, services may change, and privacy policies may change. What does this mean to you? Generally a change doesn't mean much when it gets down to the wire, unless your web hosts contracts with third parties to mine your data, or change their privacy features where they have rights to your online information. Often, with such a competitive market, companies can increase their revenue by selling your personal information.

All the above facts aren't meant to create anxiety, but rather assist you in making an informed decision. Once again, most of your top rated web hosts generally do not engage in this kind of practice.

## Paid Web Editors

You can always purchase website builders (editor) such as Adobe Dreamweaver ($400+/-), or Microsoft Expression Blend ($350+/-). There are plenty of cheaper options that deliver a great product. I have always used Microsoft's web development tools, but if you are just starting out and planning to purchase a good web editor I would recommend purchasing the Adobe products such as Dreamweaver.

Currently, Microsoft Expression Web 4, is free to download and use. This program has not always been free; it is the program I used previously and still currently use. It is a very powerful program and offers great tools for both the beginner and the seasoned webmaster who likes to code straight into CSS and HTML.

## Free WYSIWYG Web Editors and Builders

Below are a few free web editors you might look up on the web and download. All of these programs are free to use:

- Microsoft Expression Web 4
- BlueGriffon
- KompoZer - Easy Web Authoring
- SeaMonkey Composer (Mozilla Composer)
- Amaya Web Browsing and Authoring
- NetObjects Fusion Essentials
- Trellian WebPAGE

# Training

The best place for good software and third party training is YouTube – absolutely! YouTube is a goldmine of step by step instructions, practical tips, tricks, solutions and explanation of features. Google, who owns YouTube, should go down as one of the wonders of the world. Opening a new tab in your browser to Google or YouTube must become second nature. With any question, the first line of offense and/or defense is Google or YouTube.

Some programs come with very helpful documentation. Their website help areas often offer videos and even templates to get you up and running.

I do not mean to belabor this point, but YouTube cannot be underestimated. I use it multiple times, nearly every day of my life. Many larger software products have scores of multi-video training series furnished by third-party organizations. Not all the videos are fit for use, but you will figure that out soon enough.

Visit www.melvinbarnett.com for additional information, videos, and examples.

# 5 |Soliciting Archive Materials

Building a digital archive department is going to be much like constructing and acquiring artifacts for a traditional archive department which includes tangible assets. The project is going to take planning, communication, soliciting, work, and a lot of patience. Not everyone will be motivated. Not everyone will have this new venture as their top priority. This means you are going to have to wait on people to be moved. During this time you must remain focused, optimistic and very patient.

You will be dependent on people to help you gather most of the artifacts, whether they are tangible or already in a digital format. As I said, you will have to have patience, thus learning to work in other people's time frames. It may become frustrating when you have to deal with broken promises of delivery and all the excuses people will give because your archive project isn't their first priority.

Unfortunately, the treasure of the whole archive department generally lies in their hands, not yours, at least at the moment of conception. Remember to be patient, professional, respectful and thankful for the help you have and the assets that you will amass. You must show a high level of gratitude no matter how long you have had to wait or the obstacles you have had to overcome in the process.

Securing assets for your archive department whether tangible or digital will take time. But time can often play tricks and what looks like forever will be here and gone the next moment. Take steps to record as much information as possible about assets that are donated or loaned. Don't assume anything and do NOT devote only to memory any information given to you about photos, documents and/or other tangible assets; write it down. Write it clearly and document it well. Leave nothing to the imagination or memory—write it all down. Document so well that a stranger could take up your work the next day and continue without a bump in the road.

You must assume that no one knows anything about the item(s) being donated or loaned to the archive department. Therefore documentation is a must. Old pictures need to have names associated with them if at all possible. The event, location and date of photographs are important to document as well.

After you plan out your first couple of meetings, you should then consider gathering and documenting the assets. Go after the quantity of items first. Trust me, there will be plenty of hard stuff to find as times sets in. As you begin building the archive, word will circulate and excitement will breed some momentum.

When people begin to see the work you are doing, buzz will follow. Attempt to get the photos on a website as soon as you can. But don't throw something together for the sake of getting it done. The website will tell a lot about the church and those that are building it. You always want to strive for excellence. You want your work to be a reflection of the style and character of your church.

Buzz will most likely lead to others wanting to take part in this ministry. People enjoy talking about themselves and members of their family. This natural human behavior may be harnessed to ignite others to take time to look for more old photos and various assets to contribute to the archive department. You want to take advantage of this momentum because it will not last forever.

Social media sites can be a real booster if you will use them tactfully. These social sites are really good for driving traffic to your archive site, especially when you post a few old photos and tease where there are more. Instructions and warnings concerning Social media sites are discussed later in this book.

You may have to write a rule for the type of items donated. The archive department needs to be filled with assets that speak to archives of the church, institution, civic organization as a whole. What the department isn't, is a particular family's show and tell on the dime and labor of the church. You want to be careful to keep a healthy balance of material that is inclusive of the whole church instead of few members and/or their family.

Photos, artifacts and such should, in an obvious way, be centered on or tethered to the church - not someone's particular event. For example, a few old photos of previous pastors and their families celebrating Christmas in the parsonage is acceptable. Old Christmas morning photos of a member(s) unwrapping gifts isn't okay. While one person's Christmas is just as important as another's celebration, the archives is about what has made the church great as a whole. Sadly, it is human nature for some people to be more dominating than others; you must be forewarned because this behavior may rear its head when collecting archives as well.

A rule stipulating the kinds of gifts that are acceptable is VERY important. This rule needs to be spelled out from the beginning because before long you are going to receive a box of photos from some wonderful lady in the church. She will want you to use them because they are pictures of her parents and grandparents nearly a hundred years ago. While dated photos of members of the church are VERY important and should be used, you can't, however, devote a majority of photos to one family.

Visit www.melvinbarnett.com for additional information, videos, and examples.

# 6 |Labeling the Archives

Proper labeling of all archive material is absolutely necessary. While you and a few others may have knowledge of the artifacts, both tangible and digital, others do NOT. When collecting assets for an archive department you MUST document ALL items; this includes documents, photos and tangible assets. Leave nothing to memory – absolutely nothing!

The surest way to properly document is to use a tried and true means such as the MLA (*Modern Language Association*) style. It is universally accepted and proves to be complete. If you are going to create your own style, perhaps you can get some ideas from the following MLA format.

As for photographs, there are several formats - depending on what the image is used for and where it came from. Most photographs for a digital archive department will be those personally taken and donated, or loaned for scanning purposes. For all personally taken photographs you can observe the following MLA format:

Photographer: Last Name, First Name (if you know who it is).

Photograph:  Title and/or Description/Year (date if you know it).

Person(s) in Photograph: First Name, Last Name (left to right, first row to last row).


Example:  Doe, Jane. "Fall Children's Sunday School Picnic." July 12, 2013. First row: Jack Smith, Sandra Polk, Rhonda Nelson, Steve Gibson. Second row: July Gardener, Marie Phillips, George Gibbs, Frank Hinkler.

Many photographs will not include the photographer's name, and even if they did, most people wouldn't necessarily want their name listed as the photographer. In such a case skip the photographer and proceed with a title.

You might consider adding a location to your photographs. Even though most photographs may be easily identified by their surroundings, over time many changes occur. Over the years some buildings will have been modified, or demolished to make room for an existing structure. Natural markers may have changed, younger trees matured into larger ones, distorting the location. The format below may better serve the department:

Photograph Title/Description, Person(s) in Photograph (left to right, first row to last row). Location. Year.

Example: "Fall Children's Sunday School Picnic." First row: Jack Smith, Sandra Polk, Rhonda Nelson, Steve Gibson. Second row: July Gardener, Marie Phillips, George Gibbs, Frank Hinkler. 1025 Epps Street, Columbia, SC. July 12, 2013.

Or

Example: "Fall Children's Sunday School Picnic." First row: Jack Smith, Sandra Polk, Rhonda Nelson, Steve Gibson. Second row: July Gardener, Marie Phillips, George Gibbs, Frank Hinkler. Soul Harbor PH Church, Columbia, SC. July 12, 2013.

The above examples will assist you in consistent citing of all your photographs. If you have a tangible photograph you might label it on the back by writing all the information on a non-permanent label then sticking it to the back of a photograph. The most important thing to remember is, to gather all the information you can about a photograph and consistently label using the same method.

If you must write on a photograph, write on the back of the photograph, using a small point permanent marker that will NOT leave an impression.

DO NOT EVER LABEL THE FRONT OF A PHOTOGRAPH. Labeling the front of a photograph mars and diminishes its quality and appeal.

Visit www.melvinbarnett.com for additional information, videos, and examples.

# 7 |Folder Structure and Filenames

Perhaps one of the most important factors in editing photos, videos, audios, pdf, documents, etc., is organizing them in a consistent, methodical way. When it comes to building your archive system and uploading to your website, unless you employ a decent folder and file description system you WILL soon regret it. I cannot stress enough the importance of this chapter of the book. Failure to use a good system of labeling your files and folders will cost you time and heartache in the future as well as confusing those that have to go behind you.

## Photo folders and files

As long as files are being saved to the appropriate folders, the folder name and structure (tier) can be used to provide further information. When naming an individual file, stick to the details of that specific file and allow the folders above it to provide the context.

For example: in most situations, photographs should be categorized first by the year taken, then a subfolder briefly describing the event. At last, the file name should reflect the date (yyyymmdd: 20140223; or mmddyy: 022314), the event (as brief as possible: horse_show), and a number (I like to use the actual photo number given by the camera). Here is a good look at the tier: My Documents> photos> 2014> feb_horse_show> 20140223-horse_show-0211.jpg

If the folder and file names above sound a bit too exhaustive, or perhaps a little confusing - you will adapt and come to appreciate the actual simplicity, even if you can't realize it now. Stick to a good folder/file naming system as illustrated above and you will have little trouble finding your images, or any other file for that matter.

Also, when people search for images, the search engines can use the search words to find an appropriately named image file. For example, if you were searching for a picture of a 2014 Chrysler Town and Country Van, the file "2014ctnc-01.jpg" wouldn't yield in a search engine like a file labeled "2014_chrysler_town-and-country_van-01.jpg". You truly want to be as descriptive as possible without getting too crazy.

# Website folders and filenames

Your website begins with what is called a "root directory"; this is the main folder for ALL your website information. The root directory name should reflect the name of your website to some degree. If you are setting up a website for York Community Church, your root directory could go two ways, "yorkcommunitychurch" or "york_community_church".   Either one is acceptable.

There are two main components of a website, the local server (that's your computer's hard drive where the root directory exists) and the remote server (that's the hosting server you will be uploading every folder and file in your local root directory). The remote server and local server should ALWAYS match – folder for folder and file for file - hence, the importance of keeping the folders and files clean and consistent at ALL times so there id perfect synchronization.

If you are using an online web builder, normally you will be working directly with a remote server, not so much with your local server (personal computer). Even in this case, you should go ahead and set up a faux root directory where you can keep ALL website related files, such as webpages, graphics, documents, videos and photographs on your hard drive. These folders and certainly filenames should match the ones you have uploaded to the web builder. If your web builder allows you to download the site, you want to do this often.

If you are building your website locally, you MUST mirror the remote and local root directory vice versa. If you do not keep folders and files perfectly synchronized in location and name, your website will FAIL to work properly. Make no assumptions in this matter.

Now that you have a root directory it is time to go over some tips and facts about naming files and folders for websites. As technology has improved, so has the flexibility in naming files and folder. Today you can create folders and filenames with spaces, capital letters and even some special characters. However, websites are not nearly as accommodating, these conveniences do NOT work as well in cyber space.

Most remote webservers operate on a Linux or Windows based server. While Windows servers are more accommodating concerning filenames, Linux systems process upper and lower case letters differently. Linux based servers are generally more affordable than Windows. The industry has for a long time preferred the Linux platform because of standards, tools, knowledge, economics, and available personnel -along with being easier to manage; however, Windows is gaining market share.

So, whether your host server is Linux or Windows, below are a few general, and may I add accommodating, rules to follow in naming folders and files, especially for use with a website:

- Filenames and folders are case sensitive: Index.html is not the same as index.html. The homepage is ALWAYS labeled "index.html" or default.html".

- Use only letters (upper or lower case), numbers, the hyphen "-" and underscore "_" when naming files and folders. Example: 2015-special_winter_sale-01.html.

- Never use spaces in filenames or folders; replace spaces with hyphens or underscores.

- Do not use punctuation marks or special characters in folders and filenames.

- As a general rule of thumb (however, not necessary) use only lower case letters, hyphens and underscores in all your folders and filenames. Adapting this rule cuts down on mistakes and improves overall continuity across the whole website, both in the local and remote servers.

## Folder Structure

There are many basic elements that go into all websites. Their structure is important and can NEVER be compromised. Websites consist of graphics, images, html files, pdf's, documents, texts, various scripts and such. When you pull up a particular webpage your browser immediately starts pulling files from all kinds of folders located all over the root directory, as well as pulling information, scripts and graphics from other online remote sources that are linked to your website; some of them may be hosted on other servers located thousands of miles from your hosting server.

For example, one particular homepage (index.html) I recently built consists of 111 various links to files and folders consisting of graphics, Images, scripts, styles, and various links located in the root directory, as well as located on other sites and servers from around the world. This is why you MUST have continuity in the structure and names of folders and files; there is no room for error.

If all this structure sounds complicated and creates anxiety, it shouldn't. Following this book, along with some great tutorials, makes it really easy. I have learned that typically the web (html) editor is right and I am wrong. When something isn't working, it is because I have made an error.

I have spent hours looking for the error and when it came down to it I found an extra space between a "quotation mark" and/or a "less than" mark. Of course I had to look through more than 600 lines of code. To a webmaster all this is in a good day of work. To you, it may seem too overwhelming.

There is a silver lining to what can seem like dark clouds, many good web editors have special editing features built in that catch some of the errors in the code. They also come with options that let you test the integrity of your website. Best of all, generally you can fully test the website through your local server by previewing in a browser of your choosing. If you are using an online builder, for the most part, you don't worry about errors, but you are also limited in the customization of your website.

My intention isn't to create fear and anxiety, but to NOT understate the facts. From the start of this book I have been factual and forthcoming with all the good, bad and ugly.

Here is my subjective analysis when it comes to personal character and successful websites. It's never about YOU! YOU cannot afford to be stubborn; follow instruction and protocol no matter what YOU think. Build your site for others, not yourself. An error is never about what YOU think; it's about what is and isn't correct. YOU can't change the rules just because YOU don't like them.

Why the rant and why now? Good question. As I said your website starts at the root directory. From there, you will have many folders, sub folders and perhaps hundreds to thousands of files. The foundation of the website isn't the code, it's the structure. The aforementioned homepage has to retrieve files and information from 111 sources, ALL of which include folders and files, whether they exist on my server or a server half way across the world. Follow the rules and YOU will be successful!

Visit www.melvinbarnett.com for additional information, videos, and examples.

# 8 |Internet Providers & Connections

A digital archive department is as dependent on an Internet connection as it is on a computer itself. The Internet will be used to transfer data to and from your host. Once data is loaded on your host, people can search or find it by typing in your website domain.

Internet connections through providers come in a few forms that are worth knowing. Below they are explained:

### Wireless
If your location already has a Wi-Fi connection this may be all you need to have your system up and running in minutes. You will need to know the proper SSID - "Service Set Identifier" (think of it as an IP address for a wireless network) - to use if you see multiple networks appearing on your device. There is a good chance you will need a password to connect to network. Most Wi-Fi networks are secure, thus requiring a password. If they're not secure, chances are they should be. Wireless connections are configured through a router which plugs into DSL or Cable.

### Hotspots
These type connections are through mobile devices such as smartphones and certain tablets. In short, a smartphone or tablet, through paid services and/or software, creates a Wi-Fi connection from itself. A computer equipped with a wireless card recognizes this system the same way it does a typical Wi-Fi signal. Generally, Hotspots are limited and their signals are weaker.

### Dial-Up
This connection type is unacceptable if you are building a website. It is VERY slow and can cause a lot of interruptions while transferring large blocks of data to your host. A two second job turns into five minutes of waiting. If all you have is dial-up service in your area, you could consider satellite connections. Satellite prices are dropping by the month and the technology improves each day. Avoid dial-up connection unless there is no other affordable solution.

### Broadband

This high-speed Internet connection is provided through either your cable or telephone company. These connections use multiple data channels to send large quantities of information. **DSL** and **Cable** are high-bandwidth connections.

Broadband offers your best service and connection. Generally, they are fast and dependable. Many times they are discounted in home phone and cable packages. If you live in a larger city you often have multiple providers with a wide-range of options and prices. A good plan is worth researching.

> Warning: Stay clear of cheaper packages with limited bandwidth. Lately many providers are limiting their bandwidth. For example, my broadband cable bill would cost $600 - $800 under a limited bandwidth plan. There are times when every person in my house is on the Internet. There are times when there are three full featured shows or movies being played on Netflix. If you have the option to purchase unlimited data transfer (aka Bandwidth) versus limited data, this is a better option, if affordable. Data overage charges are out the roof and what many providers charge should be a crime.

### Satellite

In certain areas where broadband connection is not yet offered, a satellite Internet option is your only hope. Generally, they can be costly and I haven't seen one yet without a limited bandwidth, except during the hours of 12AM – 6AM. So, unless you are a night owl or have weird working hours this isn't practical. Generally the download isn't the fastest and uploading isn't much faster than accelerated dial-up.

While I am not a fan of the current satellite Internet providers or options, they are improving in speed and affordability. Fact is, satellite service is better than dial-up service, any day.

A word to the wise, when purchasing satellite service ask plenty of questions and READ the fine print of the contract. If you secure services and decide later that the system is not working out, or there are better options, to break the contract could cost you a small fortune. Unfortunately, I have plenty of friends that satellite is their only option, and few of them are really ever happy. Be careful!

Visit www.melvinbarnett.com for additional information, videos, and examples.

# 9 |Websites

## Domains and Hosting

**NOTE: If your church already has a website the process just got easier, just simply create a page(s) for archives and link from the homepage. Planning, acquiring equipment and obtaining assets still has to be done.**

A website is always the route to creating the perfect digital archive department for your church. There are plenty of options to choose from depending on your budget and the services you will need. The largest obstacle to having a website is finding someone to build it and maintain it, all for a reasonable price. However, today there are plenty of DYI (Do It Yourself) online web builder programs often offered by the Registrars or service providers.

Before we proceed, let's take time to clear the air on a few issues. Social Media sites such as Facebook are not websites, nor are they replacements for one—Facebook is what it is, a social media forum. Yes, it is free, but you cannot use it to build a website and store information. Media sites like this come and go. They get purchased or gobbled up by larger entities all the time, often creating new policies, changes and even deleting services - including your precious time and digital property. When this happens the fine print of the Terms of Service will reveal you have no legal recourse.

Furthermore, stay away from free websites! Stay as far away as possible. Nothing is free! If it seems too good to be true, it is. Here's what goes on with free sites. Most often two things are happening and both may be going on at the same time. First, they're mining your visitors' data and using it to solicit business from them in some form. Secondly, and most often you will see advertisements posted on the sides and even in the middle of your website. This is cheesy to say the least!

The last thing your church wants, are visitors to your new website getting pop-up warnings, virus alerts and having to meander through all the solicitations. I find that most of the solicitations are NOT very tasteful. My friend, these free websites are not trying to sell your visitors Bibles. They often use provocative photographs, to advertise casinos, ED products, and so-called hometown people looking for dates, and offer other distasteful products and services. Please invest in a paid website. Nothing is more distasteful than having to look at men and women who are available in your hometown, while visiting a ministry website.

Many free websites consist of an extension of their own domain. These domain names are difficult, stir more questions than they answer, and with a change in policy (after a quick board meeting of their stock holders) render all your printed material obsolete. And, you do not have control over what goes onto your website or how your URL (Uniform Resource Identifier) will appear (domain name: myname.com). To give you an example of my point, suppose your church is named Faith Community Outreach.

Your free website will be combined with the hosting (free) website and some random set of numbers, alphanumeric sequence and at best, a shortened version of your church name. Suppose the website Free Church Web host free sites for churches; below are some examples of what your site might look like:

- 34767.freechurchweb.com
- sk94c4.freechurchweb.com
- freechurchweb.com/45365
- fco.freechurchweb.com
- faithcommunityoutreach.freechurchweb.com

The last option is obviously the best choice that represents some recognizable domain for your church, but it's just too long and no one can remember it. Imagine this website added to your business cards and various promotional stationary?

One of the key downsides of such websites, other than the constant and often distasteful to obscene advertisements, is the replacement cost of unused printed materials. At some point you will become frustrated and figure out that the savings were not worth the trash you and your visitors have had to endure. So all the business cards and other printed and promotional items have to be thrown away. Please save yourself from embarrassment and financial waste; buy your own domain.

The aforementioned route isn't the one you want to take. Once again, spend a few dollars and invest in your own domain. This purchase will save you embarrassment and considerable time and resources in the future.

Paying someone to build a website is expensive. There are no cheap ways around this path. But, often there are people who will volunteer their time and talent to build it for you, especially if your church will foot the expenses. Sometimes these volunteers are already attending your church.

One of the greatest resources for learning how to build a website using popular programs is Googling (using the Google.com search engine) and searching YouTube (youtube.com) for how-to videos. I use YouTube all the time for such purposes. There are even great how-to series taking you through the process from beginning to end. I once subscribed (paid) to a series of web design modules. The training consisted of YouTube videos and downloadable documents and web tools. I paid about $29 for the whole course and it was worth every penny; the information I gleaned was worth 10 times what I spent.

If you have little to no experience with websites and are not very computer savvy, I highly recommend using an online web builder offered by your web host. They are usually very cheap and often come packaged with a domain and hosting service if you choose. However, before purchasing packaged products MAKE SURE YOU ARE THE DOMAIN REGISTRANT (domain owner). In other words, make sure you can take your domain to any provider of your choice if you decide to leave or transfer your business.

Many web hosts are very eager to sell you services, but transferring them to a competitor is not easy at all. They personally make it very frustrating, to say the least. Also, remember that most online web builder programs attached to a host will not allow you to transfer the website material that you have built. The only thing transferable is the domain if you are the registrant; you will have to purchase hosting and their own website builder if they offer one.

Many webhost providers only offer email support for their products and services. Do NOT use these businesses – you will be sorry.

Do business with a domain and/or hosting company that offers FREE Tech Support during business hours and even after hours if you can. Often you can get a cheap deal on hosting, but their Tech Support is via email or real-time chat... no. No! You will live to regret this decision made trying to save a few dollars over the whole year. Sadly, there are few national companies that offer tech support all day, all night, and all year. Thankfully, with the advent of nationwide coverage on most phone plans, toll-free calling isn't as big of a draw as it used to be. The webhost I use is www.ichurchweb.com; I recommend them to anyone who needs a website host.

There are two things that go into making a website work: a domain and hosting. Explain? A **domain** is the "www.mywebsite.com". The **hosting** is likened to storage for all your information that is always available to the public for visiting and downloading. Hosting is backed up on servers located all over the world, depending on how large your provider. Hosting is kind of like a 24 hour hard drive that contains all your website data that is available to the public. Fortunately, this hard drive (hosting) is located on someone else's computer instead of your own.

A Church domain is generally listed as an organization, so you would have a ".org" extension. If the ".com" is available I would purchase it as well, if you can budget an extra few bucks ($9.00 +/- a year). Owning the ".org" and the ".com" is always an asset when possible. Fact is - many people just quickly type ".com" at the end of a domain out of habit—so own both. Take the ".com" and forward the domain to the other (.org); this is usually a free service.

Pick a domain name that is as inclusive as possible; this makes it easy to remember. The three golden rules of successful websites are: "traffic, traffic, traffic." The last thing you want is a hard-to-remember or hard-to-search website. For example, if you attend New Hope Fellowship of Columbia, SC, you would not want to buy, nhfellowship.org or hopecolumbiasc.org. A better choice would be newhopefellowship.org or newhope.org or even nhfc.org. Remember to keep it as simple and as inclusive of the name as possible. Lately, more times than not the perfect domain name is already taken (purchased). In this situation, you have to be creative. Using an acronym is not taboo, but I try to steer away from doing so as much as possible.

Also, remember that your domain is often going to serve as your email extension, for example, pastor@nhfc.org. Pick something that you can live with and people can remember without too much difficulty. The church I last pastored was First Pentecostal Holiness Church of Winnsboro. Yes... too long a domain for that one. I agree. So, I used fphcw.org. It was simple and I just told them it was the acronym for the church. Be picky; this information is going to go on printed materials and also be used in search engines all over the Internet.

You can purchase domains all over the place, but I have used the same company for the purchase of domains and webhosting for nearly two decades. I would suggest using ichurchweb.com to get started.

Simply stated I look for four qualities in a service provider: Cost, Free Technical (human support, not a machine) Support by PHONE, Availability of support – 24/7, and minimum Language barriers. The only one of these four qualities that I would be willing to budge on is the 24/7 support. Under VERY limited circumstances I might be willing to move to weekday business hour support, but to be honest, after enjoying 24/7 support there is no reason to change now. Some may say why so bent on 24/7? Personally, I enjoy calling after hours and/or early in the morning - before many others get on the phone creating wait time. If I am up late and need technical support I just call and get a tech on the line in a few minutes.

Language barrier is a very sensitive subject. Let's be clear, I am not a bigot. It is my prerogative to do business with whoever I want. When it comes to technical issues, I want to speak to a person who, for the most part, speaks fluent English and moreover, if possible, in my own dialect. Technical issues can create a lot of frustration; I don't want to add insult to injury by constantly having to repeat myself and have technicians repeat themselves as well because neither of us really understand what the other is saying. This whole issue generally comes down to outsourcing. I don't care from whom or from where I am getting technical support, I just want to understand them and them to understand me.

Do not be persuaded to save a few dollars if a provider promises you personal 24/7 email or chat support. First of all, it's not personal. Secondly, when you have to wait five minutes to get a reply from your chat or an 8 hour return on your email, you will realize the mistake you have made, often over the savings of two dollars.

Purchasing these products is about you and what you want, not what the providers have to offer. There are plenty of service providers that can meet my four qualifications. I know, because I have used many providers and assisted many people in transferring away from those who didn't. www.ichurchweb.com meets all four qualifications and has other resources that are great for ministries and other enterprises.

When you build a website you want domain and hosting support that you can depend on at all times, around the clock, 365 days of the year. You want to talk with a real human, not a machine. You don't want to have to correspond through email over a period of a few days. You want to be able call them when you are having a problem, not just when they are in the office. You also want to talk with someone you can honestly understand, someone who can speak to you like a neighbor across the street.

By the way, generally speaking you're not going to have many issues with domains, once you make the purchase and get the technical details to give to your hosting provider there is little left but to renew the domain every year. I would suggest making the domain purchase for a minimum of three years, whereas hosting can be monthly, quarterly or yearly. Also, as I have stated, keep your hosting and domain support through the same company.

Hosting is the next hurdle to cross. Every website must have hosting. Either you are using their own proprietary web builder or you are going to have to transfer all your data to the server through an FTP (file transfer protocol) program. Hosting is generally divided into a few, usually three, basic plans - including unlimited hosting. Some basic plans may include a 5 page website for a few bucks a month, a 10-20 page website for a little more, and then unlimited hosting.

Domain and hosting prices are always changing. You want to look around before making a purchase. Be sure to read the reviews. Check out 5 to 10 providers and their prices, this will give you a good idea of the market.

Be careful with plans that fit a niche such as businesses that specialize in churches. While there are some good ones that are competitive such as ichurchweb.com, these niche providers are filling a market share for honest financial gain. Often their prices are higher even though they may tailor a website and a few tools toward a market. When shopping around avoid providers that cater to your industry until you get a good grasp of the market. Often providers can reduce prices.

Currently, if you are looking for a host plan that includes a web builder you should find something with about 5 pages for around $3.00 per month, 10 pages for about $5.00 per month and unlimited pages for around $8.00 a month. Often you can get this bundled with a free domain for a year. If you do not have a person that knows how to build a website, this is a great route to take; it is easy, fast and often very functional.

I have consulted with a lot of ministries that had purchased a website package, sometimes ranging up to $1500.00 up front, and $30.00 per month thereafter. Sadly all they furnished was a good selection of templates and some Christian clip-art for the price. The ministry still had to build the website and upload all the material.

When shopping around you will find that you may be able to save a dollar on purchasing a domain from one Registrar and hosting your account through another provider. If you dig enough you can de-construct every element of a good website product, but do NOT fall victim to this unfortunate mistake. It is worth a few dollars to keep all your business under one roof, if possible; the benefits far outweigh the disadvantages.

I am a big advocate of shopping around. I have gone to several grocery stores shopping for the sales and bargains, but there comes a point when your time and travel expense have to be factored into the whole savings equation. The key is to do business with a company that can provide all the great amenities at a great price, every day.

## Domain Name Registrants

One of the most important facts you need to remember is - when purchasing a domain or website package, have in writing that YOU are the Domain Name Registrant.

The material you are about to read is some of the most important information in this book. When purchasing a domain or website package, make sure you are the REGISTRANT of the domain and the Administrative Contact; you must see or have this in writing. Ignoring this information can come at a real cost down the road. Just because you set up and have paid for the website does not make you the owner. The person who owns the website is the Registrant. Often the Registrant is the web developer or Registrar of the domain.

Many website companies both local and online offer all kinds of services and products. They often package all kinds of discounts and such, but only in the fine print do they state that THEY retain ownership of YOUR purchased domain. Even though this is VERY deceptive on their part (leaving the fine print up to you to figure out, especially when many people purchasing their first domain and hosting are very confused and ignorant to the point) it is, however, VERY legal.

One of the most frustrating and costly disappointments of owning a website comes when you learn that you are not the owner of YOUR domain. When does this disappointment come? I have found that it generally occurs when you figure out that you have been getting hosed down by ridiculous high prices and/ or contract renewals and want to move to a different vendor.

These scams can be rolled up in all kinds of neatly packaged products. They appear to be very helpful and more often than not, financially sound; but, the common denominator is the Registrar remains the Registrant. In such situations there are all kinds of backdoor loading and even early transfer fees that can cost you hundreds of dollars. My intention isn't to create anxiety, but rather save you a lot of worry and financial loss in the future.

There are some so-called legitimate Registrars that I could name, but for liability's sake it wouldn't be prudent. There is an area in the book where I discuss what a decent website should cost; stick to those numbers and you should be safe. Below are a few things you should consider when purchasing a domain, hosting, website package, and even a product or service to build your website.

Any decent Registrar will give you the option of buying a domain for a year, but will likely try to sell you on the idea of purchasing it for three or more years. They often offer financial incentives for purchasing more than a year at a time, usually discounting each year anywhere from 10 – 20 percent. For ministries, it isn't a bad option to go three years. However, I would be a little apprehensive about going more than three years.

Many Registrars will roll up domain and hosting into a package deal and incentivize purchasing for more than a year- this is very common. However, All DOMAINS (not necessarily hosting) have to be purchased for at least ONE YEAR AT A TIME. If this isn't the case, there is a good chance (99%) that you will not be the Registrant; in this case you really need to read the fine print VERY carefully.

Most hosting is charged by the month, quarter or year, and can be rolled up in a onetime yearly or multi-year package, often for a really great price.

These scams work several ways; the common denominator is generally you are not the Registrant. Here's how it works. ABC Websites, Inc. is having a sale on a website package for $19.00 a month with the first two months free. There is no upfront cost. They offer free Technical support through email, and an online builder with plenty of templates to choose from. At this point the package can go several ways. First package: you can drop the website after two months and not owe a dime, just walk away, plain and simple. The second package: they will secure a credit card authorization and only begin charging after the two months is up. In both situations, they own the domain and when you find out that there are better plans available from other providers you have to buy them out to leave with your domain name.

In closing, allow me to communicate this issue a little more clearly. All the stationery, business cards, word of mouth, vendors, friends, networking with your domain and email is worthless when you leave your provider, if you don't purchase the domain from them. This is a common practice and is done legally every day of the week. I know a lot has been said about this issue, but my intention is to help you make the best informed decisions about building a digital archive department. I cannot stress the importance of doing business with a good well-respected provider. As I said, ichurchweb.com is a solid business with great prices and service, to boot.

## Online Web Builders

Online web builders can be a great way to get up and running quickly with a little hands on practice and some video tutorials. If you will follow some of the instructions and practical advice found in this book, your website can look amazing with little practice and experience. A good clean looking website coupled with lots of imagination can go a long ways and be impressive to say the least.

The largest disadvantage of online web builders is the inability to take your hard work anywhere else. Web builders generally do not support other web builders, they are extremely proprietary. If you instead use a regular HTML editor you can save all your pages, files and folders and rebuild the site in minutes as opposed to having to completely start over again.

If you do choose to use an online web builder you might want to pay close attention to save as much of the work as you can to your hard drive, if that is even possible. You also want to employ some screen shots of each page as you build and certainly the end product. These screenshots will be great reference information if something goes crazy or you have to rebuild.

Online web builders are often coupled with your domain and even hosting services, if you choose the right option. Package deals can save you some money, but be careful when purchasing the domain. There is a great section of the book that deals with purchasing domains and special deals. While many of these specials are legitimate when dealing with a reputable registrar, you can get bamboozled in a skinny minute trying to save a dime.

With some great tutorials and a simple HTML editor you can build a good website using the WYSIWYG options if they are offered. With the aforementioned option you don't even have to know HTML or CSS to produce amazing results.

### WordPress

WordPress is also a great option for building your website. It's a pretty easy (user friendly) web builder to learn to use, but it is **VERY solid**, **accepted** and **supported** by the Internet community. There are all kinds of resources including templates, user groups, blogs, bells, whistles, and gadgets you can add as well as use to assist you in building the webpages. Most of the products in WordPress are free, others are VERY affordable.

WordPress is a very powerful solution to getting your site off the ground. As I said it is user friendly, but it takes a little getting used to to manage. Bookstores and libraries offer a lot of materials, and of course, Google and YouTube are bottomless for information and great resources for WordPress.

Many domain and hosting plans support plugins for WordPress. If you choose WordPress you still need to buy your domain and hosting. Once again, don't get caught in the trap of using a so-called free WordPress domain. The word FREE on the Internet equates to their advertising, market steering and info mining on your property...never forget this fact.

WordPress is not a proprietary product like nearly all online web builders. WordPress is an open source program. Software engineers and enthusiasts are always working to build a better WordPress and make elements of the builder much better. Most of these updates are FREE and as I have already stated, others are extremely affordable.

While WordPress is considered an online web builder, it is NOT the same as other proprietary builders. It is in a league all to itself and as I have said, it has all the support you need. If I were building a website using an online method instead of an HTML editor, WordPress would be my top choice.

## Private Registration
When purchasing a domain from a Registrar, I highly suggest you consider adding private registration, or privacy protection to your purchase. This purchase cuts down on spam, solicitations and your PERSONAL information being available all over the web. When you own a domain you can simply do a WHOIS search to retrieve all kinds of information about the domain owner (Domain Name Registrant).

The ICANN (Internet Corporation for Assigned Names and Numbers) requires that private information (name, address, phone number and email) be available through all WHOIS directories. If you purchase the private registration, your domain Registrar by proxy lists their corporate information instead of your personal information. If a third party needs to contact you, they, the Registrar, will communicate with you directly. I seriously suggest this extra expense; it is peace of mind.

It is my absolute opinion that adding private registration is a no brainer. I have personally witnessed the difference that a little amount of money saved me - from a whole lot of wasted time due to solicitations of every kind. As I said, it is truly "peace of mind." However, there is a school of thought that private registration is a hoax, but a simple "whois" search reveals the truth I have written.

Some argue that private registration enables the proxy provider as the official registrar, as far as the international law goes this is correct. Opposition to my opinion is very heartfelt among many people. They present legitimate debate and offer reasons to be considered as to why you should never purchase private registration. My intentions concerning this matter is not to bring confusion in a decision you must make, but rather to give you the facts and let you draw your own conclusions.

A word of consolation, these large reputable providers would not get away with hijacking people's domains because they purchased a private registration. GoDaddy for example, serves over 12 million paying customers (as of 4.28.2013). I would feel safe with purchasing private registration with a large provider. Their bottom line is not expanded through building and maintaining websites, it is expanded through serving the needs of those building and maintaining their own websites.

I have done my homework on this subject while trying to save a dollar in the past and being the target of all kinds of market solicitations. Spend the money for private registration and cut a meal at McDonalds to save the difference... that's about the difference. Private registration is a service. It is not the same as a company offering you something free and actually owning your domain as we have discussed.

## Email

Generally, when you purchase a domain name and/or hosting plan you receive a number of email accounts (usually 5+) you can create. This is great for administrators and staff. A custom email is very professional looking and only takes a few minutes to set up. I have personally managed website accounts ranging from 5 – 500 free email accounts. Often you will receive a set amount of free emails and a block of memory for their use. It is up to you to divide the space for your email accounts.

Some registrars will give you an email (or more) with your purchase of a domain, while your hosting plan may offer even more email accounts. The number of free accounts and space truly ranges from one extreme to the next. If purchasing your domain and hosting from the same company you can often combine the accounts, as well as get special incentives and discounts. This is one of the reason I highly suggest using one company for all your website needs.

If you have a long standing email account with a third party such as Gmail, Hotmail, Yahoo, just to name a few, you don't have to abandon these accounts if you would like to keep them. Most emails servers offer free email forwarding to their customers. This allows you to receive email from any account. It really comes down to how you want to set it up. You can also have an email account auto-reply with a message that you have changed email addresses, along with other messages. I always recommend you use your domain's email account over a third party; it just looks much more professional.

When purchasing website products be careful not to get bamboozled into buying extra email packages. The vast number of people building websites don't need the extra package. Businesses exist to enlarge their bottom line when possible; Registrars are no different. If you operate a small church, ministry or small business and you know that the email space included is not enough, there is a REALLY good chance you need to look elsewhere for domain and hosting.

Email space can be a VERY legitimate problem... for medium-sized to large businesses, not the average to even larger ministry. This is why many Registrars will attempt to oversell you an additional plan. The simple solution to space issues is to learn to delete any useless email as soon as you check it. Secondly, occasionally clean (delete) your trash can. Thirdly, and often most practical - "pop" your email to start with. In other words, set up a pop email server on your personal computer. This way the email downloads straight into your computer and doesn't clog up your online email space.

When setting up a pop account you have several options to choose from. A great option for those who need to access their email from remote computers and devices - you can choose to have emails remain on the email server for a specified time. For example, I have multiple email accounts, but ultimately all of them download into a computer or device. However, for two weeks I can go online and continue to access my emails because I have all my accounts deferring the deletion of the email two weeks after it has loaded on my local (my computer) email server.

Three of my email accounts are downloaded into my Android where I delete them after I have read them, or delete them because I have read them already on my desktop. I also receive the same emails into my tablet. This is not nearly the hassle as it may sound. These emails are using a POP type server setup instead of IMAP.

There are other setups that allow you to check email on multiple systems but as soon as you read the email it doesn't download into any other device, it remains on the main (online) servers. For example if you email comes into your IPhone or Android phone, it will show it has been received and checked but remain on the server. Most people use this option (IMAP) over a traditional POP account.

Both Mac and Windows freely offer a decent local email server product, generally coupled or built to interact with a so-so calendar, task, and contact solution. I have always used Outlook which is not a free product but falls under the Microsoft Office Suites. There are also other great products on the market to use besides Mac and Window solutions.

Visit www.melvinbarnett.com for additional information, videos, and examples.

# 10 |Social Media

Social Media is powerful, influential, and it's here to stay. The objective in this chapter is to demonstrate how resourceful harnessing social media can be to your ministry, especially your media and archive departments.

Below are some talking points consisting of various facts and surveys relating to social media and various products and services.

Thankfully, most social media services are free to use. This eliminates budget restraints and frees up every one to make a contribution that will impact your church, ministry or organization.

## Social Media limitations

First, and foremost, social media apps and websites are NOT a replacement for a personal, business or ministry website! No matter how powerful, how many users, and how customizable a service is, do NOT be deceived into thinking all you need to do is post a few photos and blurbs about your church and people will be informed and inclined to attend. It's not that easy!

Social media sites come and go. They rise in popularity only to be replaced by ever demanding consumers with an appetite for more bells and whistles. Therefore, the social media market will constantly evolve due to consumer supply and demand generated and steered by technological advances in hardware and software. Dependence on social media must be limited because of the constant uncertainty of the aforementioned evolution of technology.

As the social media market evolves, social sites will rise and then fall victim to a consumer stampede rushing to the next big deal. Subsequently, advertisers will finish the kill as they move their investments, trying to head off and/or corner the market as they wait for the consumer to arrive.

Because of technological advances, unpredictable consumers, and marketing, there are too many variables in this equation to invest in anything other than a constant, which is... you. Social media is all about everybody. It's about people all wanting to be heard while having to put up with advertisers trying to lure them into spending money on their products and services.

The success of ALL social media is dependent on community. Whether its family, neighbors all living in a given geographical area, or a community of likeminded people who share common interests. The presence of community will exist physically as well as through what we now call social media. You can either be present, attempt to lead head and shoulders above the rest or recluse and go unnoticed.

## Three reasons your archive department should use Social Media Service?

### 1. Ubiquitous (It's everywhere)
Social media is everywhere! It's on our phones, our tablets, laptops, televisions, and desktops. It's even migrating into our automobiles and household appliances. Our western culture is literally addicted to social media. About the only thing that can limit social media is unfortunate interruptions in our internet and/or network connections. The number of users is astounding and the projected growth of more users is staggering.

As of August 2014, the earth's populations stands at 7.18 billion. 2.95 billion people are active internet users. 2.03 billion are active social media users. 1.56 billion are active mobile (smartphones etc.) social media users.

As of January 2014, 74% of online adults use social media networking sites; 72% men, 76% women. While 89% of younger people online, ages 18 to 29 use social media, 49% of adults 65+ who are online use these networking sites as well. Education and economic status has very little effect on users according to statistics. Of the adults online you can see the various Social Media sites broke down below:

- 71% of online adults use Facebook
- 22% use LinkedIn
- 21% use Pinterest
- 17% use Instagram

    Source: Pew Research Center, 2014; US Census Bureau; InternetLiveStats; Facebook; Tencent; VKontakte; GSMA Intelligence

### 2. It's Influential (personal, community and commerce)
As seen below, social media users play a big part in their community's economy.

- 47% of social media users are more likely to spend money on clothing and accessories.

- 44% of social media users are more likely to give opinions on politics and current events.
- 19% of social media users are more likely to attend professional sporting events.
- 46% of web users look to social media when making a purchase.
- 8 out 10 small – medium business use Social Media to drive growth.
- 3 in 5 small – medium business have gained customers using social media.
- 67% of twitter users are far more likely to buy from the brands they follow.
- Over 90% of Twitter users say they follow business to get discounts and promotions.

### 3. It's Habit-forming

Studies have shown many people cannot resist the spell of social media. While a ministry should never engage in exploiting peoples habits, the idea here is people are going to follow the information and photos uploaded to social media sites. People are going to share their thoughts concerning your posts. Based on the science cited below, when items are posted, those that are following are likely to stop and view and even comment.

- 56% of Facebook users check their account daily
- 40% of people surveyed don't mind being interrupted for a Facebook message.
- 32% of users check their social media site during meals.
- 12% of Facebook users check their account every couple of hours.

Why the habit? A recent Harvard University study showed that disclosing personal information activates the same part of the brain that gives pleasure when a person enjoys good food, receives money or has sex. Although the actual sensations are different, the study tells one that the human brain considers sharing experiences a pleasurable one – and part of being human is to constantly seek emotional and physical gratification.

Source: Liberty Voice; Social Media Addiction. Harvard Study: Disclosing information about the self is intrinsically rewarding by Diana I. Tamir and Jason P. Mitchell; Department of Psychology, Harvard University, Cambridge, MA 02138

## Social Media is not all pretty

Everything that glitters isn't gold. Social media has its downfalls too. Many would argue that everything wholesome and productive about Social media can be quickly and equally countered. It doesn't take long to find a lot of dirt and horror stories how social media has destroyed relationships, homes and even people's employment. All these facts are true. But, do you throw the baby out with the bath water? No! Eat the fish and throw out the bones. If used properly, social media can be a powerful free tool for your church and archive department

## How to use Social Media for your archive department

Some have made the argument that websites are for people who are new to a church. Social media is for those who are already engaged with a church. Here are the facts, social media is in real time, and websites are not. A new social media post goes straight out to those following. It's much easier than checking all over a website to see if anything has been added.

The key to expanding your website and social media presence is to simply exploit human nature. People are curious by nature, and most often predictable; therefore, incorporating tactics that tease people leaving them short of the whole story is good marketing and good for your successful archive department.

Thus, we use social media to stir curiosity about the archive department with teaser photos and blurbs. As things are added to the website it is advantageous to post links and a few photos to drive people to the website to see the rest of the information, articles or photos

While posts, and feedback are individually defined through catch words (tweet, like, share, etc.) depending on the particular social media platform, the response of followers will drive traffic to your website if properly linked.

The three golden rules of website success are: Traffic! Traffic! Traffic! Perhaps the three golden rules of a successful social media site are: Buzz! Buzz! Buzz! You see - in short, the tease creates buzz, and buzz translate to traffic to your website, which is the ONLY constant in an ever changing market.

So, get onboard and sign up for all the top free social media platforms; link them to your website. Invite your family, friends, co-workers, neighbors, to join, link, friend, or whatever the new catch word will be. Ask them to invite their family, friends and so forth to "join" as well.

As you add content to your website, post a few photos, blurbs and teasing information to entice them to follow a link to your website where they can spend time surfing your site free of advertisers and all kinds of distractions.

Keep your website as fresh as possible with new content, and keep the social media presence real and always linking to the website. There is no limit to what you can do to tease, create buzz and drive traffic; just keep it honest, professional, encouraging, and always glorifying to the Lord Jesus Christ.

Visit www.melvinbarnett.com for additional information, videos, and examples.

# 11 |Websites: Basic Design

The three golden rules of a successful website as stated earlier, are: Traffic, traffic, and traffic. A church website isn't about traffic as much as it is about simple, easy to find, organized information about the ministries and calendar of events of your church. If your church already has a website you can simply add a digital archive department and cut through all the website expenses. If your church does not have a website then I would suggest while building your digital archive department go ahead and create the church a website as well.

Here's the key to a successful church and/or digital archive department— easy navigation; it's a must. People must be able to navigate through your website with little pause. The last thing you want is for your visitors to become disgruntled and leave your site because they can't find information. In time, they may communicate their frustration with other potential visitors to your church.

Keep your website up to date. Do not use dated information and designs on your website. Come across as bold and fresh, not sloppy and uncaring. Visit other ministry websites and search for templates and website designs so you can maintain a current image. A cheap looking website will convey to visitors a cheap minded church. Even an inexpensive WYSIWYG builder can be made to look like it was built by a professional.

The brightest, wisest and street smart person can fall victim to a slick website. Years ago I dealt with an individual who was very savvy, and no one's fool, but the individual would fall victim to a good website every time. You want a classy website that is clean, neat, and professionally done on all levels. These kinds of websites can be created for pennies. By using FREE online tutorials, you too can create a neat, functional website.

Who you are must stick out. As much as you can save a visitor from searching, the better. Start with the name of the church or ministry. Put it at the top and make it big. Make it consistent across every page of your website. Learn how to use templates and keep the same structure and colors throughout the whole site, if possible.

The location of the church is a must. You may consider putting it right under the name on every page. You DO NOT want people trying to figure out where your church is located. And you certainly don't want them having to call the church after Googling your name to get the phone number, yet this happens all the time.

One such ministry I use to have to deal with had their post office box posted all over the website. But who wants to schedule a meeting or meet someone at the Post Office? You want a street address posted all over the site. You can post the mailing address on the contact page. Many visitors want to know the service times and address so that they can go to Google Maps or MapQuest and see how long it will take them to get to your service on time.

Speaking of a map to your church, consider embedding Google Maps into your website. With little effort and knowledge you can add a really nice script that will embed a current map where visitors can type in their address and receive directions to your church without ever leaving the ministry website.

Your service times, as well as location, needs to be posted on the homepage. Many people are so concerned with bells and whistles they forget to post their main service times, as well as other various ministry services and times. Don't make visitors to your site have to search for your meeting times. Make this as easy as possible.

Outside of clean bathrooms and a great music program, people want to know about childcare and children's church programs. Every church is at war trying to solicit or hold on to the family with young children—they are priceless in the church world. If they are an asset to your church you'd better make room and use some web real estate to let them know just how important they and their children are to you.

What you believe is important. More and more people are willing to abandon their roots in a particular denomination and explore their communities for other places of worship. People who have visited other churches inside their own denominations have realized that all denominational churches are NOT the same. These, as well as other reasons, have freed up people to visit other churches outside their denominations, and even comfort zones. This is why you need to convey your beliefs or statements of faith.

It is very important to list your beliefs and even convey your churches values.

You may even consider listing your mission statement, values and statement of faith on one page; but make it easy to find. There is no need to run from what you believe. Trying to lure people into your church without letting them know the doctrine of your church is deceitful and anyone who does this should be ashamed of themselves.

The staff of a church is important. Use web space to introduce information about your staff. A church website is about the whole church, not just the pastor or pictures of a building. It is a fact that visitors to a church want to gain a little information about the whole church, not just the name and location. Offer the public a glimpse into the lives of the associates, administrators and such.

Visitors want to hear from the pastor. The pastor may not be as important to the member of a church but for the outside world he is the single person who will best represent the church to the community. His messages and thoughts are important to individuals looking for a church.

While many are looking for a great children's program, out of this world music and talent, the sermon subjects, style and delivery will be a major factor in their deciding to stay or keep looking. For this cause, it is good to have some of the sermons online where people can download and enjoy.

Remember, the average person does not like to read - and mixed with his or her short attention span you'd better capture their attention quickly. This can be done by using more visuals than text. Keep the message simple by directing visitors to where and what time you meet from the homepage.

Keep church terminology to a minimum. Unfortunately, many people do not understand religious terms as they once did, even those who were raised in church. For example, when referring to Jesus, use His name instead of Savior, Redeemer, and Son of Man. Your goal on the website is to get information to the visitor as fast, efficiently and clearly as possible without them having to search, think, or read very much.

Make all things simple. Pay close attention to words and terminology. Assume that visitors have little to no understanding of religious terminology. The homepage, about page, contact page, calendar page, ministries page should be easy to read, spacious, clean of widgets and neat. There is plenty of room on a website to educate the ignorant, delve deep into the theology of the church and teach your heart out on the significance of the Hebrew and Greek, just don't start on the homepage, nor any of the pages listed above.

A website should be clean and neat. White or black space isn't a negative, nor is it an invitation to fill it in with clutter. You want a website that is spacious looking, just like a clean home. Clutter (that includes graphics, moving objects, etc.) isn't pretty, it's busy and suggests that an amateur designed the website. Hold off on the music as well. It's very distracting and cheapens the experience, no matter who is singing. Nothing is worse than having your children in bed, lights turned down, speakers left wide open and you finally get a chance to visit a website - only to be scared out of your chair when some hideous midi (electronic music) immediately blares when you reach the homepage. No! No! No!

Do NOT add music or loop music in the background unless the website visitor chooses to turn it on and enjoy. Below are some great tips to follow:

### Here are a few tips

- Explore other similar websites to get ideas.
- Sketch out your web design on paper.
- Choose an easy to remember domain name that best describes you in as few words as possible.
- Define goals for your website - what you want to accomplish.
- Define who you want to attract to your website.
- Understand the needs of your users and market to them.
- Create a newsletter or something to continue contact with visitors.
- Keep your pages small in file size; you want them to load quickly.
- Keep your webpages consistent throughout your whole website.
- Don't make your webpage too wide; you do NOT want people scrolling the width of the page.
- Minimize font use and use industry standard fonts.
- Don't be afraid to create and use templates.
- Add relevant content to your website.
- Keep your website content fresh.
- Have a call to action on every page. Lead your visitors to doing something or making some decision.
- Check, and recheck links to make sure they work.
- Use plenty of white (black) space. Do not clutter a webpage.
- Don't make your visitors think. Everything should be obvious.
- Remember that the human eye is trained to read left to right, top

to bottom. So, important information should follow this natural flow.

- Make the most important elements larger and easier to access.
- Spell everything correctly.
- Limit your primary color pallet to three colors.
- Webpages should match your branding. Use logos and company colors.
- Don't be afraid to sparingly use big, bold images.
- Pages need great navigation.
- Condense your menu; use sub-menus if you need to.
- Add resources. Establish yourself as a true leader.
- Pages should have contact information – phone number on each page.
- Get quality hosting for your website. You want the site to be up all the time.
- Add an "about us" page, people want to know who you are.
- Create a mobile version of your website.
- Your pages shouldn't be longer then they need to be.
- Continue to test your website.

Hopefully these tips will assist you in building a wonderful website.

Visit www.melvinbarnett.com for additional information, videos, and examples.

# 12 |Photo Sharing Services

Today there are many photo sharing services on the web and most of them are absolutely free to the noncommercial user. Not all photo sharing services are created equal, but there are plenty of good ones to choose from—shop around. There are advantages and disadvantages along with perks and services offered by most of them.

There are two reasons you might consider adding a photo sharing service to your digital archive department. If you do not have a website, nor plan to have one any time soon, you can post a lot of your photos and scanned documents online and carefully organize them for easy viewing, both privately and publicly. Secondly, you can use a service to host your photos for retrieval and online storage. You might say you are gaining a free Cloud service and extra backup system for your digital archive department.

There are six features you should look for in a great photo sharing website:

- **Accessibility:** You and others should be able to find your photos easily by dates, and/or tags.
- **Printability:** You or someone else should be able to download or order prints.
- **Quality:** Your photos should not be over compressed. They should be preserved at the highest resolution possible.
- **Shareability:** A great site will make sharing your photos across social media, blogs, and various electronic devices a breeze.
- **Simplicity:** You should be able to load photos easily and have the ability to make online edits.
- **Space:** Do they offer enough FREE space to store photos for a few years, or, is their space affordable if you need to buy more? Read the fine print. Many of these sites tease you with some free space, but once you have used it all they are simply too expensive to continue to use. The result is - you lose your pics when you leave, so have them backed up locally.

In addition to the previous mentioned advantages, you also get free sharing with family, congregation, and other friends. Many websites offer online editing, promotional products and a means to order prints. You have the availability to sort, categorize and display your photos in all kinds of creative ways. These services do NOT take the place of a good website; however, you can at least use them to begin uploading, tagging, and displaying your hard work online.

Most of the sharing sites offer a fair amount of privacy settings such as usernames and password protection. The photos can be encrypted and, because of the server types and security measures, they can't be Googled out of hiding, even if you are using advanced search filters. However, you will make a tragic mistake the day you assume anything is totally safe and fool-proof on the Internet. Never post anything that you do not want the world to see or know – NEVER!

The disadvantages of using a photo sharing website are few if you plan on putting the photos on a website. What you share publicly is public. People can copy, save, alter and repost to their own website or sharing service. Personal information attached to the photo can be harvested and possibly used against a person by a scam artist. A photo of a child that comes across as cute and innocent may prove, down the road, to be embarrassing to that individual. These disadvantages exist for a church website just as well.

Some sharing sites allow RSS Feeds. This allows family and friends to be notified when new pictures are added. This can be a great advantage for your digital archive department if you do not have a website. Folks can freely subscribe to gain this great and simple service.

When choosing a photo sharing service you might want to Google them for reviews. Some large services are used to store large amounts of pornography for website linking. You want to stay clear of such vendors, but truthfully, you cannot prevent people from posting such materials on even the best sites. The ones I have listed are NOT known to be a safe haven for pornographers, but nothing on the web is absolute.

Below is a list of the top free photo sharing websites. Before making your final decision on one, go to each site and read the terms of agreement as well as their privacy statement. Do not assume anything about the host website - what they may be entitled to and how they may use your private information or even sell your email and other information to marketers.

Please take time to do some of your own investigation and read various reviews on your favorite search engine. Be sure to give reviews their merit, but remember there are people who cannot be satisfied. I am a huge review shopper, but I have learned that you cannot please everyone. Generally a score of 4.0 out of 5.0 is good enough for me.

These photo sharing services are a great short term solution but are NOT a great alternative to creating your own website. Also, remember as we have discussed before, nothing is free. Free photo sharing sites are generally advertising, market steering or collecting data through cookies installed on your computer. Many of them honestly fail to make a real profit, but selling premium memberships and using CPM (Clicks Per Thousand) programs provide some financial gain.

### Top Free Photo sharing websites:
- Flickr
- SmugMug
- PhotoBucket
- Picasa
- Shutterfly
- Snapfish
- Photobox
- Kodak Gallery
- Phanfare
- WebShots

## Photo Rules

### Photo/Video Waivers:
Photographs and videos of your church events are some of the greatest assets to your website. A photo gallery brings a lot of life to the church. Statistically, people will view the photos and videos before they view a lot of the printed information. The old saying, "a picture is worth a thousand words" holds true for church websites and PR campaigns. People love seeing people, especially if they appear to be happy and having a great time.

You should take every reasonable opportunity to involve people enjoying all the events at your church. Laughter and visual emotions are powerful, convincing and contagious to the viewer. You don't want too much of a good thing, but you want people to see your church, not just read about your church. You want people to see your staff and congregation, not obvious stock photos out of a box.

For the purpose of building and maintaining a church website you do not need a photo release waiver signed in most cases. Keep in mind that images taken cannot be used for commercial use, rather they are used as news about what is going on in your local church. Laws vary in each state concerning the liabilities of photography and videography; however, federal laws trumps state laws, and the federal law is clear.

This issue of whether you need waivers or not was settled on March 4, 1789, when the Constitution became the law of the land. Free speech and the right to a free and independent press protects church newsletters and their websites just as it protects other news photos, organizations and major media news outlets. The use of good judgment is always in season. Responsible, respectful and obviously ethical positions must be observed.

You should always follow the following four rules of responsible journalism:

- Do not intrude into anyone's solitude, seclusion or private property without permission.
- Do not publish any private information about a person without written permission.
- Do not print or post any photo, video or story that presents the subject in a false light.
- Do not use any photo or video of any person for any commercial use unless you have written permission.

Adherence to the above mentioned rules will safeguard you and your church from a lot of issues which may lead to trouble. Never be argumentative to anyone concerning a photograph or videos posted by your church; take them down immediately, offer apologies and move on.

*"An ounce of prevention is better than a pound of cure."* So, if it makes you feel better when photographing children (ages below 18) have the parent or guardian sign a waiver. I would suggest having the form signed before you know when you will be taking photographs and keep the form on file indefinitely. A waiver is NOT a necessity.

---

**Below is a sample of the content that should be included in an Image Release Form:**

I hereby grant _(Name of church)_ (the organization) permission to use my likeness in photographs, video recordings or electronic images in any and all of its publications, including website entries, without payment or any other consideration. I understand and agree that these materials will become the property of the organization and will not be returned. I hereby irrevocably authorize the organization to edit, alter, copy, exhibit, publish or distribute these images for purposes of publicizing the organization's programs or for any other lawful purpose. In addition, I waive the right to inspect or approve the finished product, including written or electronic copy, wherein my likeness appears. Additionally, I waive any right to royalties or other compensation arising or related to the use of my image at any time. I hereby hold harmless and release and forever discharge the organization from all claims, demands, and causes of action which I, my heirs, representatives, executors, administrators, or any other persons acting on my behalf or on behalf of my estate have or may have by reason of this authorization.

I am 18 years of age and am competent to contract in my own name, or if I am under age 18, a parent or guardian has signed below. I have read this release before signing below and I fully understand the contents, meaning and impact of this release.

__Printed name__, __Signature__, __current Date__


If the person signing is under age 18 we would ask that that person sign but there must also be the signed consent by a parent or guardian, below:


I hereby certify that I am the parent or legal guardian of __Child's Name__, named above, and do hereby give my consent without reservation to the foregoing release on behalf of this person.


Parent/Guardian __Printed name__, __Signature__, __current date__

_____

**Below is some information you might want to include in your Web Site Privacy Policy.**

When using photos of __(Church Name)__ events, attendees, or members - either directly on the Website or in our photo albums - we use the following guidelines.

- We try not to post anything that would be embarrassing, objectionable or hurtful to anyone in the photo. If we know someone is shy about such things, we ask them before posting the photo.
- We don't put names as captions with photos (except for pastors/staff or other members who have given expressed written consent)
- We will gladly provide credit for who took a particular photo if desired by the photographer, and we would certainly honor any copyright wishes or restrictions.
- We will gladly remove any photo immediately upon request.

In any case, if you see a photo that includes you or your child and would like it removed from the site, we would be glad to do so. Just notify the webmaster with the details of your request.

Visit www.melvinbarnett.com for additional information, videos, and examples.

# 13 | Scanning Photos and Documents

## Scanning photographs and documents

Using a scanner will be a must in any digital archive department. It is the most practical, economical, and efficient means of digitizing all (11"x14" or smaller) images and documents. Once a tangible photo or document has been digitized you can then add the metadata to the file, and return the item to its rightful owner or properly seal the item for archival purposes.

Nearly all scanned images need to be enhanced to some degree in a photo editor. Some scanners include an inexpensive editor or a slim version of a professional editor, such as Adobe Photoshop Elements in place of its big brother Adobe Photoshop. You don't want to skimp when buying a digital scanner.

I would strongly urge you to purchase a flatbed scanner, these are not multipurpose machines; however, they do one thing really well — scan! Many of them can scan the image as well as old film slides and negatives. The flatbed scanner is the practical route to take when using it for your archive department. Plan to spend between $150 and $250 on a decent flatbed.

I use a Canon 9000 Mark II Color Image Scanner. The cost was $169.00. I researched and read many reviews before making a decision on this product. The reviews were exceptional. The features were rich and based on what I would be doing, this product would more than fill the need. There were more expensive options but I didn't want to over purchase and waste money. Make sure you do some online research and read reviews. A good place to read reviews, whether you buy from them or not, is Amazon.com.

There are other type scanners: Sheet feeders, Automatic Document Feeders, Duplex Scanners, and a few specialty scanners. Many MFC's (Multi-Function Copiers) come with a scanner feature, even a flatbed for copying and scanning. Unless you purchase a really expensive MFC you will be much better off with a dedicated flatbed scanner; they simply produce a better image! In the short run, and to save money, if your church already owns a MFC you might use it for a while to get things up and running. Then upgrade to a dedicated flatbed scanner later.

Use your scanner to scan images, not edit them. Scan at the highest resolution (DPI, dots per inch or PPI, pixels per inch - higher the better) available and then import or use your photo editing software to acquire the scan, then edit. Most decent scanners have some built in options, such as sharpen and contrast filters – don't use these options; they are not usually as good as the ones that come with good editing software.

If you want some really great scans, use uncompressed formats such as a TIFF (Tagged Image File Format) or a PSD (Photoshop Document) file. I will cover file formats in another section. I would not save files in a JPEG (Joint Photographic Experts Group) file. JPEG files are compressed and lose quality! PSD formats are slightly compressed, but this is a good trade for saving hard drive space.

Once the image has been scanned, edited, and cropped, you can then save the file for website viewing use. For printable images you want to save in at least 300 DPI/PPI as opposed to 72 DPI/PPI for digital use in a website. The file size is significant between the two and even greater contrast when saving uncompressed TIFF files. You cannot use 72 DPI/PPI sizing for printing!

> NOTE: The use of the acronym DPI has more to do with printing than it does web viewing. In this book I refer to DPI and PPI a good bit, but DPI has to do with the amount of dots of color a printer puts on a one inch area. The higher the DPI the clearer the image will be printed. 72 DPI is an older system that is still in practice today for converting images from their higher file size to a less resource hog on your memory. In conclusion, technically DPI has more to do with printing and PPI has more to do with viewing.

> Monitors (computer screens) do not see nor understand DPI, just printers. However, all images on a monitor are interpreted by their pixel size instead of inches.

You always want to scan items in color. Good editing software can change the color in an image during the editing process, but various artifacts and strange color areas can be edited and fixed once you know what you are doing. It is very hard to fix a black and white image over a color scan.

Scan documents in color, at the highest resolution (DPI), no filters, and save as a TIFF or PSD. Scan all images in at the maximum resolution (DPI), no filters, and save as a TIFF or PSD. Some of these files can easily reach 150

MB as opposed to 7 – 12 MB.

Once you have scanned these images or documents you can always edit them down to a more appropriate file size, even for archiving. Don't be surprised if you have some VERY large files when you scan; that's fine, edit and delete later.

## Digitizing Large Images and Documents

Every now and then you are going to come to a situation where you need to take a photo of a photo or document; this will require some planning and preparation. Scanning is always the best method, but because of costs and size it may not be the best route for the budget.

Using a scanner is generally very practical. But what about old documents that are bound - perhaps torn edges and other age related demise? How do you scan those items? You don't. The best way to capture those images is to use a digital camera, tripod and a stabilizing method for the image or document. If you are going to take photos of documents you must have a tripod; don't even attempt to do this free-handed, no matter how good the lighting is.

Anytime you are trying to capture documents or images for digitizing, you NEED good lighting. Do not use flash, use good ambient light; flashes often distort and blow out your target in such cases. You want the light bright and even on the subject you are capturing. In photography, lighting is as important as the subject and equipment you are shooting with. You also need an easel and something white, such as paper or poster board, for a background. In most cases you do NOT want any other background then white.

Once you get your subject situated on the easel you might consider making some marks on the poster board for centering and left and right margins, if you have multiple subjects to capture. Once you secure the tripod you can begin to set and focus your camera. If you are shooting multiple items of the same size and color you can simply leave your camera and change out the subject with each shot. Be very careful to not bump the tripod, camera or easel.

When setting the camera, you do not want to use filters and contrast or sharpening effects. Take the photos in as large a format as you can - uncompressed if possible. If you are shooting a DSLR, shoot in RAW if you camera supports it. Also, because your camera will not be too far from its subject, you want to avoid bokeh (blur) or depth of field issues so you do not want to shoot with a wide open aperture. You can always adjust the shutter speed to absorb more light if you need to, especially since you are shooting with a tripod. You may have to do some experimentation to get it right, but once you have it, you can take a lot of photos pretty quickly.

Once you have the images you can easily start the editing process and use all the filters and auto correction settings, if you like. We discuss editing software in another location of the book, but to go light on the budget you can use Adobe Photoshop Elements, Adobe Lightroom or go even cheaper and download a free copy of Gimp. If you can, add metadata to your images; while editing would be a great time to capture all the information about the image and embed it into the file. See Photo Metadata.

Visit www.melvinbarnett.com for additional information, videos, and examples.

# 14 | Editing Photographs

## To be, or not to be on the website?

Each photo in your archives represents your church or organization. Every photograph or document on display represents someone's consent to exhibit it. With this in mind you want to be mindful of the subject you are posting. Frankly, some of this is common sense, but occasionally a pic slips through the cracks.

"The camera takes what it sees," those words sparked the first fight between two girls I had ever seen. Yes, those words are true, but what the camera sees doesn't have to be displayed. Below are a few simple rules to follow:

- Never use a photo that represents anything negative about a person or presents the subject in a false light.
- Consider their posture, is it pleasing?
- Are the people improperly exposed for the moment? Make sure pants, skirts and sleeves are down, necklines and collars are up.
- Are the facial expressions acceptable for the situation?
- Does the subject have something noticeable on their clothes or body, especially their face?
- Will the photo draw attention to a person and cause them to be mocked?
- Does the photo express emotions that the subject would not want others to see?

## Critiquing Photos

If you are going to build a digital archive department, you, or someone will have to assume the job of judge and perhaps jury of what a good photo is and if it should be used, filed or discarded. Generally, this task is not too hard, but there are some great pointers that will help make your presentation go from so-so to excellent.

Many of the photographs that will be added to your collection will come from contributors and most of them will not have been taken by a professional photographer. It becomes the job of someone(s) in this department to decide what they will or will not use. While most of these judgments are more subjective than objective, there are some great rules and standards to employ in this task.

In photography, critiquing can be divided into three categories: technical quality, composition and subjective appeal.

Technical quality can be judged by asking and answering four questions:

- Saturation: Is the color bright, vivid or dull?
- Exposure: Is the exposure (image) too light, too dark or just right?
- Focus: Is the subject in focus? How is the depth of field? What relationship is there between the foreground and background?
- Lighting: Is lighting quality acceptable for the subject?

How is the Composition? Composition moves beyond the objective to the more subjective view of the photographer and persons viewing the photograph. Good composition can be measured in three questions:

- Subject: Where is your eye drawn, to the center, a particular corner? Was the rule of thirds employed?
- Framing: Should more or less space have been captured with the subject? Is the photo orientation (landscape or portrait) appealing for the cropping?
- Balance: How is the subject vs. foreground, middle-ground, background and alignment (crooked)?

How is the Subjective Appeal? This critique separates the indelible photographs from typical ones, those that attract our attention, and those that are soon forgotten or passed by. The critique is purely emotional, but can be examined in three questions:

- Narrative: Does the picture tell a story?
- Emotion: How do you feel when you look at the photograph?
- Connection: Did the photographer connect with the subject?

If you will truly employ the three categories discussed above: technical quality, composition and subjective appeal, you will have a great gallery for folks to view. A gallery that will leave an impression on visitors as well one that will provoke their curiosity to come back again and again.

# Three Powerful Photography Tips

Below are three tips that will produce a better photograph for the beginner. I use these rules nearly every time I take pictures. There are certainly many other tips in photography, but I personally know these simple to follow tips will improve the novice photographer the first time they employ them. The idea behind these tips is to make your archive pictures look their best, and that starts with the person behind the camera, not the equipment.

## Rule of Thirds

The rule of thirds is one of the most powerful composition techniques in photography. Using this elementary rule can improve the subjective appeal of just about any photo. The rule can be used in all types of photography to produce images which are more appealing and better balanced. This rule is not ALWAYS practical, but it is a good starting point to creating excellent photos with amazing composition.

The rule of thirds involves dividing your subject using 2 horizontal lines and 2 vertical lines, as illustrated below. Think of it as a hash tag, or full frame Tic-Tac-Toe board. You then position the subject(s) in your scene along those lines, or at the points where they intersect.

The idea is that an off-center composition is more pleasing to the eye than an image where the subject is dead center of the frame. Adapting the rule of thirds into your photography or editing will significantly improve your images overnight. Below are examples of this rule.

 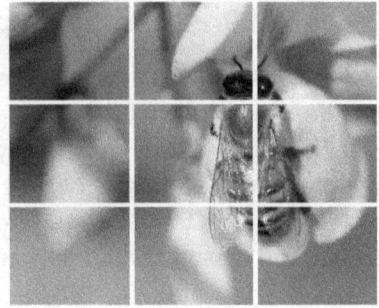

## Perspective

What do you see when you look at most candid shots? You see the subject, but from what perspective are you seeing the subject? Typically you see the subject in the snapshot looking up while the photographer is looking down. The camera is about 5 to 6 feet off the ground and 4 to 10 feet away.

A decent photograph is all about the subject. When you incorporate good perspective into your photography you bring the viewer into the inner circle of the subject. Perspective is letting the subject dominate the photograph. The images below illustrate good perspective which creates stunning images that subjectively captivate the viewer. The viewer gets the sense that the subject is now more personable and even touchable.

The four illustrations below are classic examples of good perspective. Adding this tip will significantly improve your photography and create more interest in your subjects.

## Bouncing light

Photography is all about lighting. Any person who can harness and dominate lighting through the lens of a camera is a master photographer. Most people just depend on the auto settings on their point-n-shoot or even their DSLR.

Bouncing light is hard to do with most inexpensive cameras but it is possible if you can set up for a shot. However, if you are using a DSLR and an external mounted flash you are in luck. When taking photos take time and explore pointing your flash toward the ceiling and allowing the flash to reflect off the ceiling back onto your subject. When standing against a wall taking a photo, turn your flash toward the wall and let it reflect back into the front of your subject.

Most people using flash photography overexpose and create harsh lighting for a portion of the subject and/or create a much undesired contrast between the subject and the background. Simply bouncing light can eliminate many problems and make images appear as if they were taken by a professional. Below are a three examples of bouncing light with no tripod or special lighting; all three are candid shots.

Simply incorporating the three tips I have listed will turn mundane shots into stunning photos. All three tips can be used immediately without much practice and even more...the purchase of additional equipment. For more information and detailed examples try doing a search or visiting YouTube.

## Editing Workflow

Below is a very simple workflow for editing images to put on your website. A professional photographer would use a more involved workflow that is very extensive and detailed. Once you master this simple workflow you can increase the steps as you desire. Below is the workflow I use most of the time.

### Select photos
In a generic image viewer go ahead and rule out all bad photos; delete them from your computer. A bad image has no reason to be left on your hard drive unless the image or subject cannot be replaced. Keep a clean hard drive by sorting through images and deleting the bad ones. Deleting bad photos upon import (from camera) is a really great habit to get into.

There is no rule that says you must use every photo that you deem worthy to keep from deletion. The only thing worse than having way to little photos is having too many.

Once you have made the selection of photos you want to use for your photo gallery, you must now edit them. Those you have chosen to keep but not use can be edited later. I have hundreds of photos I have kept but are not edited, perhaps they may never be edited, but I chose to keep them anyway.

### Critique the image(s)
Once you begin to critique the photos, some of them will prove to be unfit

for use, so discard them as well. But, remember that many photo editors can assist in saturation, exposure, and even lighting, so be careful not to throw out what can be edited. A bad subject, poor framing, and unbalanced photos will be hard to fix, so unless it is a priceless piece – chunk it.

Last, but not least, consider the subjective appeal - does your image tell a story? How does the image make you feel? Does the image connect with the subject? If the answer is no, you may consider deleting it unless the photo is one that cannot be replaced or modified. Obviously there are many photos that will not have subjective appeal, but are needed for a gallery or some other critical area. If you have the option to select through many of the same photos, searching for more subject appeal is the best route.

### Import your image
Now is the time to choose what photo editor to use to produce your galleries or individual photographs. In the basic workflow below, I will be using Adobe Photoshop Elements, which I would highly recommend for its quality, user friendliness and affordability.

If you are using RAW images go ahead and make initial corrections such as basic exposure, temperature, contrast, color correction, and sharpening. If importing JPG's which will most likely be the case for 90% of users, you can do this easily by using all the editor tools at the top or side of the monitor screen.

### Image tweaks
If you imported a JPG image, then you want to do some color and contrast editing. Many editors have auto filters; some are good - others are not. You can play around with them and just undo what you don't like. Here you can adjust light, shadows, contrast, saturation, and so on. I generally always add some saturation to my images. I want them to appear rich and vivid.

Using filters and other editing features can be really fun and ultimately create spectacular images, if you have an open mind and creative imagination. However, you must realize most photos need little effects added. Most could use a little more saturation and ALL of them need sharpening if taken with a digital camera.

### Resize image
Determine how large or small you want the image size in pixels (px) or inches ("). For website photos I generally crop at 5" x 7" (480px x 672px), 8" x 10" (768px x 960px), 10" x 12" (960px x 1152px) or 6" x 12" (576px x 1152px) depending on the subject and framing. There is a lot of debate over

using the 96 or 72 DPI, or just sizing it to whatever dimensions you want.

Remember, DPI is more of a printing term than an image web viewing term, but while inside a photo editing program the use and function of DPI is still largely used.

Let me digress a moment to clear the air on a much debated topic – DPI and PPI. If you Google this subject you will find all sorts of information on this debate. Simply stated there is a lot of confusion on the subject of DPI and PPI, but I will attempt to give you a simple understanding and would highly suggest you do some searching for the nuts and bolts, if you desire more understanding.

In this book I discuss that all things are digital in the computer. All digital matters use Bytes which are multiplied and make up binary code etc. Images are digital. While DPI is digital - in the computer/printer the results are visual, not digital. The accepted DPI for printed images is 300 or higher...period! 300 is not accepted because of the technology, it is accepted because of the visual quality, or science of the human eye.

In the digital universe viewed through a monitor, the human eye cannot distinguish between lower DPI's and higher ones such as 300 DPI. However, the human brain and wallet can quickly distinguish between an empty or filled up hard drive and a fast loading as opposed to a slow loading webpage.

If you want to post images that people can right click and save the photo for printing, then you want to save the image at a high quality and use at a minimum 200 DPI, but I would suggest 300 DPI. These are going to be large files!

With all due respect, most people do NOT print photos off the web as they casually browse. If you want to make all or most of your photos printable you will have to crop and save to a high resolution.

For the rest of the world, choose your dimensions, 5 x 7, 8 x 10, etc., and save as a JPEG to an image quality of about 7. This will yield you a great image for people's viewing pleasure. Just remember - the monitor and web editor it deals in pixels rather than inches.

My argument is all about file size. I don't want a file size to be larger than it has to be. File size and the amount of bandwidth determines how fast or slow an image loads, and how much room you are taking up on your host server as well as your local hard drive.

Below are examples of an image sampled at different resolutions and DPI, but cropped the same across the board. The first image sample is in RAW. This is an unedited photo as it was saved right out of my Canon SLR.

RAW format: 11.68inches x 7.78inches at 300 DPI. This image is unedited and printable. Image size: 6.88 MB. Below the image has been cropped and edited. Take notice of the extreme contrast in file sizes.

Now we will crop the image at different physical sizes, using different DPI, and variable image qualities.

Image Size: 8 x 10 inches or 768 x 960 pixels:

JPG Format: 8 x 10 (768x960) at 300 DPI, cropped, edited, printable and saved at high quality (12). File size: 3.73 MB.

JPG Format: 8 x 10 (768x960) at 72 DPI, cropped, edited, non-printable, and saved at high quality (12). File size: 320 KB.

JPG Format: 8 x 10 (768x960) at 72 DPI, cropped, edited, non-printable, and saved at medium quality (7). File size: 78 KB. This latter edit is best for website use, but not printable use. This image will load fast, take up minimum space and look stunning. Below is the same photo resized even smaller.

Image Size: 5 x 7 inches or 480 x 672 pixels:

JPG Format: 5 x 7 (480x672) at 300 DPI, cropped, edited, printable and saved at high quality (12). File size: 2.11 MB.

JPG Format: 5 x 7 (480x672) at 72 DPI, cropped, edited, non-printable and saved at high quality (12). File size: 152 KB.

JPG Format: 5 x 7 (480x672) at 72 DPI, cropped, edited, non-printable and saved at medium quality (7). File size: 51 KB.

When I edit photos for a website I use 72DPI at medium quality; this setting is usually 7 or 8. What is the difference between 7(med.) or 12(high)? Just look above and you will see. What is surprising is there is practically no difference in quality to the human eye. To see the difference would take a professional editor.

It's easy to get caught up in majoring in minors. You want to avoid these pitfalls. Consider the data above and format your images accordingly. You will have a fast loading website without any sacrifice to what is seen by the human eye. If you want to share a printable photo, then document it as so and load accordingly. Yes, it is okay to format and load all printable images, but it comes at a cost in space and speed.

### Sharpen the image

Every digital image must be sharpened. Use your Unsharp Mask option; this option gives you three settings, amount, radius, and threshold. For a web image at 72DPI, I always set the amount at about 100 to 200, the radius to .2 to .5 and the threshold between 0 and 3. For printing set the radius to about 1.0 – 1.5.

### Label the photo

The last thing I do is label the photos. Many of the photos will have no or very limited information. It is a great practice to digitally imprint the photos with critical information that will identify the subject(s) along with other important details of the photo. You can also embed metadata as you save the photo. Refer to the section on Metadata and Labeling Photographs for more information.

I suggest taking time to label each photo, if possible. The amount of information you want to add is up to you and may be relative to the photo or its use.

Use the editors Text feature to label the photos. Decide what font, size and color to use. I highly suggest using a simple and easy to read font such as Arial, Verdana, Tahoma or Times New Roman. There are few times you will ever want to use crazy fonts for archive purpose.

The size of font should be no larger than it has to be. A good way to determine this font size is to view the photo at actual size and adjust the text size accordingly. Remember the image is what you want to stand out, not the label. I prefer to place the label at the bottom right of each photo if possible, which is not always the case. You do not want to hinder the viewing of the subject. There are plenty of times the label will have to be placed to the left or even the top corners. Attempt to keep the information on one line. The reasoning behind the placement to the bottom right corner has to do with the natural flow of the human eye and how it gathers information.

As for color of text, I generally incorporate three styles. The first color of choice is always white, then black, and last if needed a custom color. The label never needs to compete with the subject(s). The photograph is what is worth the thousand words, not a label. Depending on the dominating color or shade of the photograph at the corners, use white or black. You do want the label to contrast - making it visible.

Most of the time after I have chosen the appropriate color of text, I use the layer transparency feature to squelch down the visibility of the text. At this point you might consider using the shadow or simple outer glows to enhance the label to make it clear to the viewer.

Occasionally, I use a custom color to label with. When I do this I like to use the eyedropper to select a dominant or variation of that color to use. This method is purely subjective. The idea is much like the one artists use to select matte color when framing a picture.

There is great section of this book that addresses how to label photos. You might want to familiarize yourself with this section again, or before you label your photos.

### Save image

For websites you want all graphics, including images, saved as "GIF", "PNG", or "JPG". An image is generally always saved as a JPG, especially if it is a photograph, whereas some graphics are often saved as other formats such as GIF or PNG. The key is to balance quality with file size. Most editors have a preview so you can see the image as you determine its quality. I always start at high and slide the image toward low until I see the quality begin to diminish, then I go up a notch and save the image there.

Choose file name and location. All your images should be stored on your computer and a backup system before uploading them to the website. File names and location is VERY important. You need a filing system in place before you even begin editing. See the section on file and folders.

### Upload image

Now you can use your web editor or online builder to upload images to your website.

This completes the basic workflow of photo editing. This is the system I have used for many years and it has produced some great photography and websites.

## Photo Metadata

Adding photo metadata to an image is the latest greatest thing to digital photography, and any image you have scanned. Many photo editing software programs allow you to add metadata such as copyright, captions, keywords and other vital information concerning the image itself. Metadata is not visible like watermarks and captions printed on the face of the image;

it is embedded into the file. In a nutshell, metadata is the digital version of writing on the back of a photo.

Most digital cameras store metadata on each photo. For example, my professional Canon DSLR gives me the make, model of my camera, shutter speed, aperture, focal length, ISO, date the picture was taken and even other details about the image; this extra information captured by digital cameras is called EXIF data(Exchangeable Image File Format). This information can be very useful in learning how to properly operate your digital equipment.

Two of the most commonly used formats of metadata for digital images are: IPTC (the standard developed by the International Press Telecommunications Council), and XMP (Extensible Metadata Platform developed by Adobe).

Including metadata in your images can be very helpful in properly labeling your image as well. Through using photo metadata, you can add all the necessary information you would use labeling the photo for archival purposes. Once this information is embedded in the image you can easily retrieve it through various popular image viewers such as: Windows Photo Gallery, Windows Picture and Fax Viewer, Microsoft Office Picture Manager and many others.

Surprisingly, there are a few freebie programs pre-installed on Windows PC units such as XP, Vista, Windows 7, and Windows 8, as well as the paid professional editing programs. You can also easily embed metadata with programs such as Windows Picture and Fax Viewer (Free). Apple offers programs as well.

To view metadata in an image, you can generally right click the image, scroll down and left click on properties. If you have the image open in an editor you can search around for properties, file information, photo properties etc... and view the various metadata. Not all photo editors have this function; if it supplies metadata there is no promise it will allow you to edit or generate additional metadata.

To find out if you have a program that allows an editing feature, most of the time you can right click on a photo and choose "open with"; this will generally furnish a list of all programs you can use to edit and/or view a photo. Once the editor is open, choose search for photo information and click the appropriate area to pull up this information. Once the metadata is pulled up you can choose several tabs and generally, if the software allows editing, fields will be provided where you can type various information about that image and then be given the option to save or continue.

Windows Picture and Fax Viewer, which came on some older PCs offered this snazzy viewer which allowed you to add a lot of metadata to an image. Once the image is open, right click inside the image, scroll down to the bottom of the window and left click on properties. Then left click the top tab that says summary, there you can add a Title, Subject, Author, Keywords and Comments. Then click apply followed by OK. The new metadata is recorded to the image.

This metadata will remain embedded through multiple saves and filename changes. Emailing the photo will not hinder the integrity of the metadata either.

A great use of metadata is adding it to all photographs that you are uploading to the Internet to create your website. However, many website editors will not capture and transfer the metadata onto a thumbnail, but this is no surprise and is really not needed.

This process can be a bit time consuming, but with the right software and practice you can include it in your editing workflow. Some of your professional software such as Adobe Photoshop Lightroom ($150+/-) will allow for batch insertion of metadata. Once embedded your image has all the information to ensure not only will the image be available for many decades or longer, but the information about the image will survive intact as well.

I would strongly advise any archive department to use photo metadata to ensure the integrity of the photo's information as well as the quality of image. A mere image without the story will be meaningless to the public and forgotten, in time, by those who cared. If you are just getting started in creating this type of archive system for your church you may find some programs, as I have previously mentioned, which can save you a little money. If you have lots of photos and documents to scan you might consider spending a little money and going with a program like Adobe Photoshop Lightroom. This program alone will give you incredible image correction features, filters, and color enhancements that make this program a real asset. Lightroom is powerful software used by professional photographer's every day.

## Enhancing your Photographic skills

The greatest source for enhancing your photography is online. I have spent countless hours reading blogs, forums, watching videos and then putting my own camera equipment to work trying to duplicate. I have learned a lot - while learning there is so much that I still need to learn. As a result of my quest to master photography as much as I can, I have found YouTube a blessing in every way imaginable. YouTube has truly been the greatest single source of my photography skills.

In addition to YouTube, there are some really great free classes online if you search for them - as well as sharks promising the moon if you will buy their program or set of classes. Some of these classes are VERY legitimate, others are scams. Be careful of programs that boast big promises. Personally, there is plenty of free information available if you will search for it.

Another way of enhancing your photography skills is joining online photography forums where you can submit photos for peer reviews. I have joined a couple of these in the past and received many good critiques. The peer judging can be harsh, to say the least, and often you have to suck it up and not take the criticism personally—it can be VERY harsh. The secret is to weigh it out and for one moment consider the advice of your peers. In some cases the criticism is going to be unrealistic.

Photographers can be very weird people; they often live in a strange world where little details dictate their moods. In every picture details are magnified and nothing goes unseen--nothing goes unnoticed. Examine in order to learn and never take the critique personally; let it be a challenge to do better. When, not if, you are personally attacked just pity the person and say a prayer for them.

### Be warned!

Many photographers enjoy strange and often provocative art; Christians generally refer to it as pornography. There are way too many forums that would be a great resource if it were not for the inundation of people using pornography every chance they get. While much could be argued as being tasteful and just showing the beauty of the human body, it is what it is – pornography.

If you go to any photography forum and see anything that shows nudity or anything that is considered provocative it will only get worse, so blacklist and move on to another site.

Visit www.melvinbarnett.com for additional information, videos, and examples.

# 15 |Editing Audio Files

Many churches have old cassette recordings of services from the past. These recordings can prove to be a real goldmine if you can gather enough information on the tape and get it into a digital format. I can't tell you the times I have ran across boxes filled with old cassette and VHS tapes of yester-years services.

Digitizing both audio and video for your archives is a wonderful asset. The process isn't too hard nor costly. It does however take up some time. You must see this time as an investment.

Many of those old sermons will be a real treat to hear as well as a continual blessing. With today's technology those old messages can live on as well as the legacy of the minister. Often buried in those boxes of tapes and various videos are baby dedications, weddings, special moments and some really old familiar faces that have gone on to make heaven their home.

## Convert Cassettes to MP3
Converting old audio cassette tapes is a very simple process that only requires about four items. I discuss the process below:

### What you will need:
- Cassette player
- Computer with sound card and input jack
- One male to male 1/8-inch jack cord or RCA to mini-jack cord
- Audio software

### Steps to converting:
Each computer make and model may differ. Certainly every audio software program will be different, but the workflow is basically the same. Below are simple instructions on how to preserve those cassette tapes into a digital format.

- Start with cleaning the head(s) of the cassette player. Do a search for directions – it's easy! If processing old cassettes I would do this with each cassette; it takes just a moment and can make a huge difference in quality.

- Plug one end of the mini-jack cord into the headphone or line-out jack on the cassette player and the other end into the line-in on the sound card on the computer.
- In Windows, go into your control panel and make sure your line-in source is checked. Then check your software to see if the audio input is setup. Make sure the output is set to go through your computer's sound card. Mac software is different but the workflow is the same
- Make sure music is set to record in stereo (voice recordings don't have to be in stereo).
- Under the quality setting, you want to set the sample rate high. For good quality set to 44,000 Hz.
- Press the play button on your cassette player, and press the record button on your software program. You should hear audio coming from your speakers. At this point you want to check your input recording level, this can usually be seen on a meter. Make necessary adjustments and then restart the recording. Make sure to run a few tests. Document the test and process as you create or go through the workflow.
- Write ALL the settings down, document everything, then you can use the settings over and over if the quality of the cassettes doesn't differ too much.
- When your recording is finished you will need to save the audio to your hard drive by going to the File Menu and making your selection.
- When the audio is saved to the hard drive you can further edit and convert to an MP3 file.

## Creating voiceover and adding music to your MP3 (digital) file.

In order to add voiceover and music to your audio, you must convert the audio to a digital format. If your audio is already on a CD, DVD, or any type of memory device it is already in a digital format.

All digital formats must be imported into your audio software and generally laid down on an audio track before adding voiceover and other audio such as music.

### What you will need:
- Microphone

- Computer with sound card equipped with a mic jack.
- Audio software.
- Music (royalty free) that is NOT copyrighted, or that you have gotten written permission to use.
- Small mixer board (optional).

Each software program is different, but the process is always much the same. Once again, a search on YouTube will yield some great tutorials to get you started.

You can use a selection of mics but usually they all have to go into your sound card through a 1/8" jack. You can use a typical handheld mic with an XLR jack as long as you can convert it to a 1/8" jack. Using a small mixer board is optional. Often you can use the computer software to adjust the input such as equalizing, adding reverb and other filters to your voice. With a small mixer board, you can do all this externally and feed the sound you want straight into the audio program through the jack.

If you want to add music, such as an introduction, you MUST use non-copyright, "royalty free" music. The only other way is to get written permission to use music from the owner or recording studio. The fastest thing to do is go online and in your favorite search engine type in: "royalty free music" or "free stock music".

Here's some good advice. Find a jingle for your intro and use it...all the time. Use it each time you produce another audio file to upload for your archives. It is unprofessional to use all kinds of music for an introduction to the same speaker or church program. The idea is to have a theme song and stay with it.

The other option to "royalty free" music is to find a theme song and purchase it. There is plenty of "royalty free" music online that is for sale at a reasonable price, you just have to look for it.

## Producing an Audio Message

Gather information about the message for labeling and adding voice-over. You will want to open a word processor and type out exactly what you want to say. The subject is in third person. Document to speak, not to read. You want the introduction and exit information to be clearly annunciated and sound like you are speaking to the public, not reading out of a book. Rehearse the voice-over piece several times to get it right.

Consider the important information you need to add and use this as a template for the other recordings. The point is to inform the listener what he or she is about to hear. Names, dates, places are all important information. Often you will lack good information, in such cases provide what you can and move on to the next message or event.

To produce a great audio message you will need four audio tracks that you will have add, edit, and make cuts to. This is not too difficult to do, but the first few times is not a cake-walk. Some practice, trial and error will get you in shape very soon. Expect the first few sermons to take a while. Once you get familiar with the editing software and work-flow it will be as easy as riding a bicycle.

### Message Track

Import the audio feed that contains the main body of material you want to produce such as the sermon. Depending on the editor you use, this process will vary. However, the audio must be loaded from the hard drive or directly from the media such as CD, DVD or Flash drive.

Once the audio is laid on a track you need to make edits to this specific track. Go ahead and make proper deletions of any preliminary sounds, transitional points, or dead air space you want to delete from the beginning. It is also, a great idea to go through the audio and delete any long periods of dead air space. You might also want to listen and consider cutting out any portions of the service that for whatever relevant reason shouldn't be heard.

Go to the end of the message or event and trim off any excess audio. Upon the completion of the service audio should end. Special prayer, announcements and private altar time that has been recorded should all be trimmed.

Using filters and compression settings, you can scrub the audio of unwanted noise such as hiss, background noise and various audio signals that can contaminate your track.

Audio compression most likely needs to be applied at this time. As a speaker raises and lowers his or her voice the modulation signal will vary. Depending on the editor you are using you can adjust the signals to capture a steady audio level that is pleasing to the ear. I always attempt to keep the audio levels between -12dB and -6dB. The only way to master this process is trial and error. If you take the time there are some great tutorials online and those tailored to their editor of choice.

### Introductory Track

After you have documented your introduction you want to record straight to the track using a microphone. You want to cut out all outside noise and adjust the gain so you only pick up the voice of the narrator. Once recorded, trim off ALL dead noise and adjust the equalization of the recording until you are pleased with the voice.

You want to avoid dated material in both the introductory and closing track. You want to give the ministry website in both opening and closing tracks. Save most of the information for the closing track and remind listener to stay tuned until the end of the message to find out more information.

### Closing Track

This is a very important track; you want to thank the visitor for taking time to listen to the program. This is a time you can quickly summarize the program, give directions and website to find other great programs as well. You can also invite them to your church or organization with address info. Be cautious about giving dated material such as particular upcoming events.

### Introductory Music

This is a very important decision to make. You need to carefully pick the intro-music to represent your broadcast. I strongly recommend using the same jingle each and every time. This piece of music must be free of copyright protection unless you have purchased rights or have written consent from the producer, record company or artist to use it.

If you do search online there are plenty of royalty-free or stock music websites. Read their terms of agreement very carefully. Shop around for prices because they can vary a great bit.

This music should start at the volume of the introductory track and slowly fade softly into the background as the announcer introduced information about the broadcast. As soon as the announcements are finished the volume needs to increase for a few seconds and then reduce and fade into the message track.

### Closing Music

Whether you are using the same music for the intro music or not this music should slowly fade into the message track for just the last few moments of the broadcast then increase in volume before fading as the closing track is applied. When the announcer is finished the volume should increase a few moments then slowly fade away, thus ending the broadcast.

## Final Edits

This broadcast needs to be polished and come across professional. Go over the broadcast and make all the tweaks, you don't get a second chance. Listen to the voice over, the music fades to see if everything blends well. The volume needs to be as constant as possible. You do not want people having to adjust their volume during the broadcast nor do you want them having to turn down the introduction because it is overbearing.

Once you have completed a few broadcasts this process will get very easy and will take little time to produce. I can't express how seamless this broadcast needs to sound as well as being consistent with other broadcasts. Again, producing a broadcast from some old sermons isn't a laborious project once you get a system in place.

## Saving the broadcast

If you are creating multiple broadcasts from years gone-by you need to adopt a system for a file name. The file name can serve as the Item number as well. This will make things easy for inventory purposes and also if people order a hard copy of a program.

A good simple system for filename and item number is incorporate the speaker's name and date along with the service. Use the first letter of the speaker's first name and the first two letters of their last name. Then use a six digit date system (mmddyy), followed by a hyphen and number of service or distinguish PM from AM Service. Example: MBA042215-A. There are other ways to name files, but the one I have given for an example is simple and methodical.

As you save the broadcast you will want to save it as a Mp3 format. This is a very stable format that works across all platforms. Also, document all settings from beginning to end so you can successfully reproduce programs.

Visit www.melvinbarnett.com for additional information, videos, and examples.

# 16 |Cold Storage

Most archive departments have plenty of boxes filled with items such as old photos and various documents. As time goes by these items will slowly decay if they are not properly stored. Improper climate and light will expedite their deterioration. Also, improper plastics and paper sleeves, binders and containers will inflict damage over time.

The best climate is one that is between 65 – 70F with a humidity of 35 – 50% with little to no light, except when needed.

Plastic enclosures made from uncoated, pure polyethylene, polypropylene or polyester are great for storage; they are stable and non-damaging to photographs. Avoid PVC plastics. PVC generates acids which can fade the photograph in time. Use acid-free natural fibers when possible.

Visit www.melvinbarnett.com for additional information, videos, and examples.

# About the Author

Melvin Barnett has been ministering the Word of God since 1986. Through the years Melvin has served in ministry under many titles. From serving as Senior Pastor to serving in Christian media as the Executive Producer of Christian television programs.

Melvin began ministering the Gospel at the age of seventeen. He has a Shepherd's heart and distinctly enjoys teaching the Bible, evangelism, and one-on-one encouragement.

Melvin is a native of Alabama and now a resident of Lake City, South Carolina, where is serves as the Conference Administrator and Director of Media Operations for the South Carolina conference of the Pentecostal Holiness Church, Inc.

He is married to Darlene Barnett; they are the proud parents of two precious children, Christopher and Gracie. As for enjoyment, he greatly loves being with family and making new friends. While he enjoys traveling, he also likes easy days around the home with his wife and children.

As an author he has written several books.

Melvin Barnett can be contacted at www.melvinbarnett.com